# iCope

ISBN: 1470176629
ISBN-13: 9781470176624

Printed in the United States of America

# iCope

## STRESS MANAGEMENT FOR TEENS AND YOUNG ADULTS

**Anthony R. Ciminero, Ph.D.**

# *Preface*

Stress is a popular topic because it impacts all of us regardless of age. Extensive research has been conducted on the serious effects of stress on our health and well-being. Much of the research is highly technical and cumbersome to read, but still important to our understanding and coping with stress. In earlier versions of this book, I attempted to present the *fundamental* knowledge and skills needed to cope with stress on a day-to-day basis in order to help prevent the devastating and life-threatening risks associated with stress when left uncontrolled. I have again chosen to review in this book what is essential for a clear understanding of stress and how it affects us without going into extraneous details on the subject.

I have focused on the four primary coping strategies rather than provide the reader with dozens of procedures. This book teaches an efficient approach that is relatively easy to learn. Once mastered, the procedures can be used within minutes to **manage,** but not **eliminate,** stress. As is true with any self-help book, there are certain limits to what this or any other approach can do for you. If you are having serious concerns or problems, and the use of this book or other books does not result in significant improvement, it is recommended that you consult a professional.

The first edition of one of my books, *One Minute Stress Management*, was published 25 years ago. I have kept the basic approach and

of various concepts related to stress management. Coping is an active process where we can rise above the day-to-day issues that we face. Stress, like gravity, inevitably brings us back to our normal state. Also, social relationships are important in maintaining our *resilience* to the everyday impact of stress, and their joyous leap vividly demonstrates this principle.

Many people have helped with various stages of this project over the past several years. I thank all of you for your assistance. Special thanks go to Jessi Ciminero, Matthew Ciminero, Gabby Zadoff, and others who made very helpful suggestions on the manuscript. Matthew was also particularly helpful in the final stages of the manuscript preparation. I would especially like to thank my wife, business partner, and colleague, Joanne Bauling, Ph. D., whose creative ideas, feedback, extensive input, and continued encouragement on this and prior manuscripts have contributed immensely to this final product. I thank all of you for your help.

Anthony R. Ciminero, Ph. D.
August 14, 2012

# Table of Contents

# CHAPTER 1

## *Understanding Stress*

Most of us have a general idea of what stress is. This is not surprising since all of us experience stress in some fashion throughout our lives. If you try to define stress, you most likely would identify some of the key concepts related to it. Without any training, you will know something about stress and possibly how it affects you personally.

Many teens and adults describe stress as feelings of tension, pressure, frustration, or anxiety. Others mention the physical components such as an upset stomach, tight muscles, increased heart rate, and perspiration. Still, others will describe stress as the things that cause our stress: The day-to-day events and problems at home, work, or school, as well as the unfortunate events in life such as the loss of a relationship, death of a loved one, physical injuries, parent's divorce, moving to a new school, etc.

All of these descriptions are correct to some degree in that they touch on some feature of stress. However, none of these descriptions is complete. Before we can get into the key coping skills, we must first have a more complete and accurate idea of what we are dealing with - **stress**. Learning these basic principles now will enable you to be more successful in using the techniques covered in the rest of the book. Learning stress management without a good idea of how stress operates is difficult. This first section of the book will teach you the basic principles that you need to know in order to use the iCope methods. Once you learn the basics of how stress works, managing stress will become much easier.

## UNDERSTANDING THE BASICS

Although it may seem simple, the following model is actually rather sophisticated and supported by decades of research. *Stress is a combination of various physical and psychological reactions that occur whenever some demand that requires some kind of action by the person is placed on an individual.* Obviously, these demands can range in seriousness from minor irritating situations to severe traumatic events. Regardless of whether the stress is mild or severe, there are certain processes that take place fairly consistently between the time the demand occurs and when the person takes some action to deal with the stress.

To keep things as clear as possible, we can break down the model of stress into four basic components. Familiarize yourself with these four elements in the following diagram:

# THE BASIC MODEL OF STRESS

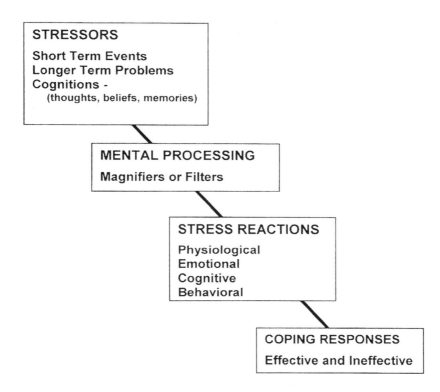

## STRESSORS

Looking at the diagram of the stress model, first notice the "demands" that are placed upon us. These demands are generally referred to as **stressors** and include any events, problems, or situations that have an impact on you. Stressors can be short-term events or they can be long-term ongoing problems that require continued attention. Here are some basic facts about stressors:

1. **Anything can be a stressor.** Some are short-term situations that pass quickly, whereas others can be chronic and last for long periods of time. Some stressors can develop into a specific phobia so the

mere sight of a dog or getting on an airplane can elicit a very strong reaction in individuals who have these fears.

2. **What is perceived as a stressor for one person might not be a stressor for another** - different strokes for different folks. A social event like a party will be great fun for some individuals, but for others this can be a very stressful situation.

3. **Stressors differ in their severity and importance**. Having a significant medical problem will generate much more stress than having a quiz in one of your classes.

4. **Clusters of predictable stressors are likely to occur in the decade between adolescence and young adulthood.** These major stressors include adapting to peer pressure, establishing acceptance in your social networks, developing your first significant intimate relationship, handling the end of a significant relationship, responding to academic demands, and setting the initial steps in your college or career path. In addition there are specific events such as parents divorcing or a significant illness/death of a close family member or friend that can occur during these years.

5. **Both positive events, such as those related to "success," and negative events can be stressful**. For example, making the varsity team at school could be stressful and add demands to your life just as getting a poor grade on an exam would also be stressful.

6. **Stressors can occur in your day-to-day environment** (e.g., tests, a conflict with a close friend, losing your keys, etc.) **or they can occur in your mind** (e.g., thinking about something difficult such as a relationship that ended, or worrying about an event such as a big exam). Mental stressors including our *beliefs, thoughts, worries and memories* can produce *as much* stress as the stressors that occur in our environment.

7. **Having too many stressors** *at the same time* **will create higher degrees of stress.**

8. **Learning how to handle stressful life events earlier in life seems to build better resilience to handle future stressful life events.** Although being *overwhelmed* by stress at any time is **not** helpful in strengthening resilience, having some challenging life events can make us stronger.

## MENTAL PROCESSES

The second major element in our model of stress includes certain types of **mental processes**. Whenever a stressor occurs, our mind reacts almost like a computer to process what is happening. Processing the information helps us know what to do or how to react. Many times the mental processing is so automatic that we are not even aware that it is happening. Therefore, much of this mental processing seems to occur *unconsciously*. Although we do not need to know everything about how these mental processes work, we do need to be aware of a few things. Probably, the most important principle to learn here is that some mental processes seem to work as **"magnifiers"** of a stressor. In other words, an event or problem will appear more serious and demanding which in turn makes the stress reaction more severe. Essentially, our minds often are programmed to make mountains out of molehills.

Many of us can think of someone, maybe our self, who reacts to most events out of proportion to the real situation. People who magnify their stressors on a regular basis tend to be more emotional in a number of ways. You do **not** have to be a "drama queen" in order to blow things out of proportion. Many people are more anxious and worry much of the time because of this process. They may be susceptible to other strong emotional reactions such as anxiety, depression, feelings of helplessness, or anger. These individuals might also have a nega-tive attitude and have difficulty seeing things in a positive light.

Other mental processes seem to operate very differently. In contrast to the **magnifiers**, these processes act like **"filters"** and keep us some-what protected from the stressors that we confront. These "filters" help us keep things in perspective and help us avoid overreacting to situations. This is beneficial to our physical and psychological health when stressful events are perceived in the most benign way possible. Even though we are all capable of using both *magnifiers* and *filters*, our culture seems to steer us in the direction of magnifying stressors.

A very important concept to grasp is that these mental processes **can** be changed. Even though mental processing seems so automatic, we can become more self-aware of these reactions and actually learn how to modify them. In this way, we can take control and reprogram our *mental computers* to minimize *magnifiers* and build in protective *filters*. The ability to change our mental processes is encouraging and will be a major coping strategy discussed later in the book.

## STRESS REACTIONS

The third major element in our overall model of stress includes the various reactions we have when confronted with a stressor. These **reactions** are rather complex, but can easily be understood when we look at all the possible ways in which people respond to stress.

There are four primary types of stress reactions: **physiological, emotional, cognitive**, and **behavioral**. As we discuss these components of stress reactions, you probably will recognize some of your own patterns. These stress reactions are part of human nature and there is no way to prevent them completely. It will be helpful for you to become familiar with your particular response to stress. As you read the following summary of these different aspects of the stress reaction, check to see which ones affect you the most.

## Physiological Reactions to Stress

Each of us has inherited a certain physiological response to stressful events. Try to think of this as the way we are hard-wired for stress. This automatic reaction is referred to as the **fight-or-flight** response which has had survival value for humans as we evolved. Essentially, our body gets prepared to handle a stressor **as if** it were an emergency or life-threatening situation. It is what most people notice in intense situations and what they might describe as feeling their adrenaline flowing.

In reality, there are many biochemical changes occurring, some of which result in adrenaline and other stress hormones like **cortisol** being produced. A lot happens at a basic physiological level. Heart rate speeds up, blood pressure increases, blood vessels in the hands and feet constrict as blood is retained in central portions of the body, and muscles tense throughout the body in preparation to fight or to flee the situation. Other physical manifestations of this *fight-or-flight* response include perspiration, reactions in the digestive system, changes in breathing patterns as well as other less noticeable effects. Again, all of this occurs naturally as part of our biological stress response.

Although the intensity of this physical reaction will differ depending upon the nature and severity of the stressful event, it is important to recognize that a physiological reaction does occur *at some level* to all stressors, including minor ones that are in no way life threatening. In essence, our bodies react primitively and respond to some degree *as if* we were Neanderthals facing saber tooth tigers or other life-threatening dangers.

Obviously, most of the stressors we face on a day-to-day basis are not life threatening, but our bodies still respond with the fight-or-flight reaction. Over thousands of years of socialization, humans (or at least most of us) have learned to inhibit or suppress overt expressions of the fight-or-flight response. Certainly this is necessary for any society to survive, but there is a price we must pay for our civilized behavior, including the physical damage stress does to our bodies. Even though we all have a generalized physiological reaction as part of our stress response, we do have some weak links in our system that can break down under stress. Those who have a lot of gastrointestinal reactivity to stress are prone to ulcers, colitis, irritable bowel syndrome (IBS), and other irregularities such as constipation or diarrhea. Those with predominantly cardiovascular reactions might be more susceptible to heart attacks, high blood pressure, vascular headaches, and other similar disorders. Because muscle tension is a major part of the physiological reaction to stress, tension headaches, TMJ (joint pain in the jaw), lower back pain, and fatigue are often associated with stress. These severe effects are easily noticeable. Other more subtle physiological and biochemical changes also occur under prolonged stress. For example, there is growing evidence that our immune system, which protects us from everything from the common cold to cancer, is adversely affected by chronic stress. In addition, there is a direct link between stress and its emotional components that are described below.

## Emotional Reactions to Stress

Our emotions or feelings such as *anxiety, anger,* and *depression* are closely tied to our physiological reactions to stressful events. Although we differ in our ability to discriminate one emotion from another, there are very common emotional reactions that almost all of us experience to some degree. For some people these emotional states are transient and pass quickly. For others, certain emotions can become a dominating feature of their life. One of the most common emotional reactions is **anxiety** or its more intense relative - *fear*. **Anger** and feelings of *hostility* or *resentment* are also common emotional responses to stressors, especially those of a frustrating nature.

When we think of the fight-or-flight response discussed earlier, it is easy to see the close correlation between the angry/hostile feelings that could lead to fighting (aggression) and the anxiety/fear reactions that might lead to fleeing or avoiding the stressor. Since our stress is often due to other people including family and friends, aggressive or avoidance behavioral patterns can easily be established in our social relationships. If someone gets stuck in a long-term stressful condition with little control over the situation, **depression** can become the primary emotional reaction.

Upon deeper analysis, research has found that the emotional component of the stress reaction is a bit more complex. Although the *physiological* reaction is quite automatic, it appears that other information is needed for us to **"know"** how to feel *emotionally*. Researchers have not found a specific physiological reaction that is consistently connected with each specific emotion such as anxiety, anger, hostility, depression, etc. Instead, it appears that while our bodies react physically, **our perception** *of the situation or* **our interpretation** *of what is happening is what controls our emotions.* This again ties into the mental processes discussed earlier, since they closely influence how we interpret any stressor. In other words, even though our body is going through the identical physiological reaction, we could feel different emotions depending on how we *interpret* the situation. Going on a roller coaster can be very exciting and fun for one person, whereas others who see the ride as dangerous are more likely to feel fear and anxiety. Stress, like beauty, is in the eye of the beholder.

What causes us to interpret things in such different ways? As was mentioned earlier, the mental processes we have learned over the years are significant. These mental patterns are strongly influenced by those who raise us and train us in cultural standards (e.g., parents, teachers, religious authorities, etc.) and by our own past experiences. If you are taught to see things in a negative manner, you could have a tendency to interpret most events - good, bad, or neutral ones - in more negative ways. You might be rather pessimistic and overly critical of yourself and others. Depending on other factors, you might be a generally fearful or hostile individual. Overall, you are likely to be more stressed by day-to-day events. Fortunately, by engaging in stress management you can learn to change some of these negative perceptions that make you more prone to stress.

The key point to remember here is that your emotions can be quite different depending on the way you see or interpret events. Later we will go into the details of how you can tune into your emotions and begin to control them by changing some of your interpretations/perceptions. Below is a list of words that describe common "emotions" in our culture. Look over the list to see if any of these are occurring too often or too intensely for you. If there are any strong patterns of negative emotions, it is important to become more aware of when and how these emotions are affecting you. Common emotions include: **anxiety, fear, depression, sadness, anger, resentment, guilt, disgust, jealousy, excitement, hostility, joy,** and **happiness**.

## Cognitive Reactions to Stress

In addition to the physical and emotional reactions, stress also affects our "cognitive" abilities. *Cognitive reactions* include any of our higher mental or intellectual processes such as our thoughts, attitudes, attention, memory, and decision-making processes. Our mind, like our body, also reacts to stress. In some stressful situations, our mind seems to be going a mile a minute, whereas at other times we simply cannot focus on our daily events. We could be worrying about an event or just trying to decide what to do about a problem. Under high stress, we can be somewhat confused and our judgment might be impaired. One of the clearest examples of a cognitive reaction to stress is the tendency to worry excessively about a situation that does not necessarily warrant that much concern. Because our cognitive reactions can be disruptive, accident rates increase during times of heightened stress. Therefore, extra caution may be needed when we are highly stressed.

## Behavioral Reactions to Stress

The final way in which we respond to stressful events includes various behavioral reactions. Some of the most typical examples are tapping your feet, pacing, biting or picking at your nails, wringing your hands, clenching or grinding your teeth, playing with your hair, or other similar habits. As with the other reactions, being aware of your particular behavioral responses will be useful later in learning how to reduce stress more effectively. Noticing your unique behavioral, physiological, and emotional reactions will be an important skill to learn.

## COPING RESPONSES

The final element in this comprehensive model of stress includes our "*coping responses*." Each of us will learn to cope with stress in various ways. We have already consciously or unconsciously devised a way to deal with stress. You may be asking yourself, "If I already have a way of coping, why am I reading this book?" The answer is probably that the ways in which you cope right now are not working as effectively as you would like. Another possibility is that the amount of stress you are dealing with at this time in your life is much greater than at other times, and you need some additional skills to help with the extra demands. A final answer is that some of your coping responses are actually creating other problems. Some coping methods have a tendency to backfire on you. Take a look at the list below to see if you regularly use any of these *positive* or *negative* coping responses.

# Potential Coping Responses

| | |
|---|---|
| Having a drink | Using drugs to feel better |
| Becoming aggressive | Smoking |
| Eating | Escaping the situation |
| Yelling at parents | Punching a wall or door |
| Sleeping | Daydreaming |
| Participating in a hobby | Watching TV |
| Relaxing | Looking at things positively |
| Playing video games | Texting a friend |
| Talking to friends | Talking to yourself |
| Exercising | Expressing your feelings |
| Solving the problem | Reading this book |

You may be surprised by some of these coping responses. However, a coping response is anything you do that helps manage your stress. Therefore, using alcohol, drugs, sex, or food can be used to deal with stress. Clearly, many of the coping responses are not very healthy or adaptive when used excessively. The difficulty with some of these troublesome coping responses is that they do work, *but only temporarily*. Some of these methods are so common and popular because they are very quick and easy to use. Unfortunately for some people, coping methods such as using alcohol or drugs, overeating, and/or avoiding problems will create even further distress in the long term. In this way a person can get trapped in a vicious cycle where stress leads to some unhealthy quick-acting coping mechanisms which in turn create even more stress.

In contrast to the ineffective or maladaptive methods used to combat stress, there are some very effective stress management strategies that will be the primary focus of this book. These methods take a little more effort to learn initially, but they will work for you in the short-term as well as in the long run. Unlike the maladaptive coping responses, the iCope methods will not create additional problems or stress for you. The main objective of this book is to teach you those additional adaptive skills so that you will have more choices in how you handle stress effectively in the future.

# CHAPTER 2

## *Ground Rules for Stress Management*

Before we discuss the four core methods for stress management there are some important reminders to help keep our expectations realistic and to help us benefit from the procedures. There are **10 ground rules** to review. If you are eager to begin learning the first two skills prior to reading this chapter, it is okay to simply read the 10 highlighted headings below and move on to the next chapter. However, it is recommended that you read this entire chapter before reading Chapter 5.

### 1. You can never eliminate stress.

Each one of us is under some level of stress every moment we are alive. Even while we sleep we can experience stress such as in our dreams. However, the intensity of our stress levels can range from mild to very strong. Never being able to eliminate stress is not necessarily bad since certain levels of stress can be positive and actually help us function more effectively. Our goal is to *manage* stress rather than to *eliminate* it. When stress is too high, you want to lower it so it does not interfere with your activities or health. If your stress is too low, you might feel bored, listless, and without energy. In these situations you might need to increase your arousal to energize yourself. You have probably seen examples of this at sporting events when a team huddles together before a game and tries to increase their intensity. Individuals might also exercise to increase their overall physiological arousal, or talk to themselves in a way to get *"psyched up"* for some event. These are all examples where more stress can be energizing and beneficial.

We frequently hear of people who have *"burned out"* or are exhausted from too much stress. The opposite can occur when there is not enough positive stress in one's life, and things can become very boring and unrewarding. Again, the important point to remember is that you can never eliminate stress. The most you can do is to manage it effectively. Remembering this basic point will keep your stress management goals realistic.

## 2. Stress can be positive.

Having the right level of stress can be stimulating and exciting. It is generally when our stress is too high or too low that we become *distressed*. Each of us has an optimum range of stress where we feel good and function well. Good stress management will require us to find our own personal **effective stress zone**.

## 3. Stress is a universal part of the human condition.

The third ground rule is that we all have the biologically built in *fight-or-flight* response. This reaction serves to warn us when we are under some level of stress or danger. Because the response is a rather primitive one, we frequently feel this way even when there is no serious life-threatening danger. Our bodies still respond **as if** we were in some real danger.

Although we all experience similar fight-or-flight reactions during stress, each of us has a "favored way" of responding. For example, many people are cardiovascular responders and might have an increase in heart rate or blood pressure. This cardiovascular *reactivity* is very stable across different situations (Lovallo, 2005). Other people appear to respond with more gastrointestinal activity than any other reaction. These individuals will notice the changes under stress initially in their stomach, which might start as butterflies in the stomach, heartburn, or similar kinds of discomfort. Still, others are muscular responders and will notice muscle tension, frequently in the muscles around the head, neck, jaw, or lower back.

## 4. The intensity of your reaction is related to the intensity of the stressor.

Minor events will trigger mild stress reactions that might be imperceptible to many of us. However, when there is a highly intense or threatening stressor, the reaction is strong and almost impossible to ignore. Almost everyone can remember these experiences when you feel the adrenaline flowing and your heart pounding. Although minor stressors produce a less intense reaction, it is not advisable to ignore these physiological signals all the time.

## 5. Some individuals have generally higher levels of stress.

Variations in our general reactivity to stress are due to a combination of factors including some that may be genetically determined. Some individuals are generally more responsive to stress, partly due to their own personality and partly due to biological factors. Very stressful ongoing situations at school and at home as well as other environmental factors will also contribute to generally higher levels of stress. The important principle to remember is that if you are highly stressed most of the time, you can learn to manage it in order to minimize its negative impact on you. If this is the case for you, it will be in your best interest to take some preventive measures to help insulate yourself from the detrimental effects of too much stress.

17

## TYPE A BEHAVIOR

*One personality factor that was linked to high stress is the* **Type A** *behavior pattern. Type A behavior is characteristic of individuals who generally seem to be very competitive, some- what hostile, energetic, and often involved in multiple activities – think Ari Gold from the HBO series Entourage. These intense individuals usually have a strong sense of time pressure and time urgency which frustrates them easily when they have to wait in lines or do other activities that they perceive as "wasting time."* **Type B** *personality is a much more relaxed style with the absence of the Type A features. Earlier research suggested that Type A behavior was associated with cardiovascular disease. However, research has not been consistent in finding this link between Type A behavior and cardiac problems.*

*However, there is some support for a relationship between heart disease and a cluster of negative emotional states, name- ly anxiety, hostility, and hopelessness. This has been referred to as the* **Type D** *(i.e., Distressed) personality. This personality pattern includes those with heightened levels of the negative emotions* **and** *a high degree of social inhibition. Preliminary findings suggest that those with a Type D personality and its many stress-related components may be predisposed to heart attacks. This may not seem like such a big issue for teens or young adults; however, the earlier you can begin to correct, or at least moderate, some of these personality factors, the better your chances are at preventing future medical problems.*

**6. Although you might not be able to change or eliminate a stressor from your life, you can control your stress reactions to some degree.**

This sixth ground rule emphasizes that even when you do not have complete control of some stressful events, you can do "something" to minimize any negative reactions. Most people generally will admit that there are numerous events over which they have little or no control. These uncontrollable events can include relatively minor irritations such as being late to school because of traffic to more serious aggravations such as a difficult teacher. Even though you cannot control the traffic on the way to school or the personality of another individual, you can learn to minimize your reaction to those stressors.

**7. Stress is cumulative and can build over time to have detrimental physical and emotional effects.**

If you ignore stress, it will eventually catch up with you. Your health will suffer when faced with prolonged high stress levels. You can experience some of the specific physical disorders (e.g., ulcers, high blood pressure, severe headaches, etc.) or you might find your resistance lowered to various diseases including common forms of the flu. The ability of our immune system to fight serious diseases like cancer can be affected by intense stress levels over lengthy time periods. In addition to the detrimental effects of prolonged stress on our health, our emotions are also highly susceptible to stress. Our emotions can become sensitized if we ignore too much of our stress. Under these circumstances it is often the minor stressor that becomes the last straw to break the camel's back. Whenever small events cause an overreaction, we must ask ourselves if there is an accumulation of stress that we are ignoring.

**8. Effective stress management requires a well-balanced arsenal of strategies rather than any singular technique.**

It would be nice if there were one method to control stress, but this is just not feasible or realistic. Each individual must develop a variety of methods to be used at different times and in different situations. The iCope techniques include various methods that can be used quickly and effectively whenever they are needed. The combination of techniques is designed to give you greater control of stress in a variety of different settings. Many people will find a few methods that work best for them, but it is still helpful to be familiar with the other options because they could be useful at different times. The iCope methods will help supplement your personal arsenal of methods to combat high stress levels.

**9. Each of us already has developed some preferred ways of coping with stress.**

Unfortunately, the ineffective coping methods such as aggression, withdrawal and avoidance, or the use of alcohol, drugs, cigarettes, or food to relieve stress, can become the easiest to rely upon. Fortunately, **all** of us are capable of learning more effective stress management skills such as those taught in this book. This takes some initial patience since you have to break old patterns while learning the new ones. Eventually you can begin to rely more on healthier new methods.

**10. Effective stress management is a skill that can be learned by anyone who has the ability to read this book.**

Like any other skill, stress management requires that you practice the skills on a regular basis. With practice and reinforcement, the skills will feel more natural over time. Much of your reinforcement will come from "feeling better" and the "sense of control" you will have over your stress level. You are likely to continue using these techniques because these methods are quick and efficient if you have practiced them regularly.

# CHAPTER 3

# *Basic Skill Number One: Self-Awareness*

A nyone who drives a car knows the importance of having basic information about how the engine is performing. For example, it is helpful to know that the engine temperature and oil pressure are normal. Most cars have one of two ways of letting you know how things are performing. One method uses a set of red lights that come on when the temperature is too hot or the oil pressure is dangerously low. The other method uses a set of gauges that give you fairly accurate feedback about what the temperature and pressure are at all times so that you know when things are running well or when a problem is developing. Do you see any advantages to either of these systems? To give you a hint (if you have not already heard the expression), the red lights are often referred to as *"idiot lights."* When the light comes on, it is often too late to do anything about the actual problem. The engine may have needed antifreeze or oil due to a leak, but you find out about the problem too late, frequently when you are stranded out on the highway. Having gauges in your car is safer and more helpful. With gauges you can see when a problem is developing, and take some preventive action to correct whatever is going wrong.

Unfortunately, when it comes to stress, many people of all ages in our culture operate with *idiot lights*. The stress has been tuned out and ignored until the stress levels reach the boiling point. When this person finally experiences so much stress that it cannot be ignored, the person is at a big disadvantage because of our basic fight-or-flight reactions. It is much more difficult to bring stress under control when the intensity is so high. Because stress is cumulative, it is easy for things to build to the point where small events are enough to cause an overreaction (*idiot lights on*).

There are many advantages for the person who maintains their own internal stress gauge system. Primarily, you would be able to learn where your **effective stress zone** lies. This ***zone*** *is the level of stress at which you perform at your best*. You would also know what levels of stress are too high or too low for you. When you recognize that your stress level is increasing to an uncomfortable level, you could then take some simple preventive steps to return to your optimal stress level. Similarly, if your stress were too low, you could take some corrective action to increase your arousal and motivation. Another major advantage to putting yourself on a gauge system is that you get feedback about how successfully you are managing your stress.

## HOW TO GAUGE YOUR STRESS LEVEL

The first and most essential step in the iCope strategies is to be able to recognize changes in your general stress level. It will be important for you to be able to ***rate*** your stress reactions accurately so that you are aware of even minor changes (increases or decreases) in your stress level. As you become more sensitive and aware of your stress, you can use these awareness skills as soon as stress begins to build. You will also be able to recognize when you are successful since you would notice whether your stress level actually changed in the desired direction. In essence, this would be comparable to having your stress on a gauge system.

There are two steps that can help you become more aware of your stress and gauge it accurately. Remember, this is your individual gauge so do not try to compare yourself to others. First, imagine a stress scale that goes from **1 to 10** (there's no zero because you always have some level of stress). On this scale a **1** is very relaxed and calm, probably what you would describe as "no stress." For many people, a **1** is comparable to the relaxed state you feel just prior to falling asleep. A **10** is the maximum amount of stress you could experience. Although many situations might feel like an 11 or 15, this scale only goes to **10**. Try to imagine the worst and most distressing event you have had to handle. Remember what it felt like? This is **your 10**. Look at Figure 3-1 and try to get a *mental image* of this scale. After you have thought about the stress scale and what the different levels mean to you, answer the following questions.

### Figure 3-1. Basic Stress Scale

**1  2  3  4  5  6  7  8  9  10**
**Very Relaxed    Alert    Very Stressed**

1. Right now, as you're sitting there reading this book, what is your stress level? _____
2. What was your highest stress level today? _____
3. On *average* what was your stress level yesterday? (To get an average rating, use two values such as 3-4, 5-6, 7-8, etc.) _____
4. On *average*, what was your stress level over the past week? _____
5. Try to think about what your stress level generally is when you are performing at your best. On average, what would you rate as your *effective stress zone*? _____

In order to become more accurate in your ratings, you will want to ask yourself, "What is my stress level?" **several** times a day. The Stress Control Biofeedback Card™ is a very helpful device to remind you to rate your stress throughout the day (Order cards at **http://www. icope.co**). Whenever you notice some distress or tension during the day, stop and rate your stress level. Over a period of time you will find yourself fine tuning and adjusting your scale as you become more sensitive and aware of your stress level. This is perfectly acceptable. If you find yourself almost always having the same stress rating, then you probably are not discriminating the different levels as accurately as you could. You can't always be a 5!

## FINDING YOUR EFFECTIVE STRESS ZONE

Take a look at Figure 3-2, which is very similar to the prior figure. Use this scale to picture your **effective stress zone.** Your answer to question #5 above will provide some indication of what your zone is. You want to know where you function at your best and have that zone as a goal when you are managing your stress. If you function extremely well in the 5-7 range, you will want to try to keep your level in that range in order to perform well. Everyone has his or her own zone. In fact, you may have different zones for different activities (e.g., at school or home, in athletic competition, in certain interpersonal situations, etc.). Most sport psychologists teach competitive athletes to keep their arousal in their zone as a basic skill in managing their stress in high-pressure situations.

Figure 3-2. Stress Scale and Effective Stress Zone

## EFFECTIVE STRESS ZONE

—————————————————————————————

—————————————————————————————

**1 2 3 4 5 6 7 8 9 10**
**Very Relaxed    Alert    Very Stressed**

As was mentioned earlier, some people operate well at higher stress levels whereas others do better at lower levels. Try to be aware of your personal tendencies and use that knowledge in establishing reasonable stress management goals. Again, you are not trying to <u>eliminate</u> stress, but simply working to <u>manage</u> it so that it works for you and not against you.

At this point, it is very possible that you do not know where your **effective stress zone** is. That's okay for now. If you do not know, hopefully you will in the near future. As you pay attention to your stress level over the next few weeks, try to note what your stress level is when you are performing very well. Try to observe the relationship between your peak performance and your stress level. The stress level at which you function the best is likely to be your **effective stress zone**.

Once you have a good idea of what your zone is, use a highlighter to color in that section of the double lines on Figure 3-2. Again, try to get a clear ***mental picture*** of the scale and your personal effective stress zone in your mind. As you confront stressful events you will want to recall this image: 1) to help you rate your stress, and 2) to know what goal (zone) you are striving to achieve.

## TUNING IN TO YOUR STRESS REACTION

In addition to building in your personal stress gauge, there is a second exercise that can help improve your self-awareness. As you recall from the basic description of stress, part of your reaction is a physiological response. Unless it is a very intense reaction we are likely to ignore it. Having a physiological reaction is very helpful because our body is *signaling* us that some action is needed to deal with the stressor at hand. Instead of ignoring these signals, we want to tune into them because they provide useful information that will help improve our stress management skills.

Although physiological reactions (*signals*) occur throughout the body, remember we often have a "favored" way of responding such as gastro-intestinal, cardiac, or muscular activation. If you are aware of your *typical response*, you can tune into stress and do something about it more quickly. This is like resetting your internal "radar" to detect the physiological component of stress as soon as possible. Complete the following exercise. It will take about a minute to find out what your early warning signals are.

## EXERCISE 3-1

1. After reading these instructions, get into a comfortable position, preferably in a reclining chair or lying down.
2. Take a couple of deep breaths and exhale slowly. Relax as much as you can, and close your eyes.
3. Imagine as clearly as you can a stressful event, preferably an **8** or **9** stressor for about 20-30 seconds. Try to re-experience the event as vividly as possible.
4. Pay close attention to your body. Try to notice any changes that occur while you are imagining the stressor.
5. After the 20-30 seconds, open your eyes, sit up, and write a brief description of your physical reactions on a piece of paper.

## Do not read the section below
## until you have completed Exercise 3-1.

When you imagined the stressor, it was likely that you induced a stress reaction including certain physical responses. Hopefully you noticed some of these. Some of the most common early warning signals are:

a) tightness or tension in the neck, face, jaw, throat, shoulders, or back;
b) changes in breathing patterns;
c) heart rate speeding up;
d) queasy feeling in the stomach; and
e) perspiration or sweaty palms.

If you had any of these reactions, they are likely to be your **early warning signals** that some stressor is impacting on you and it is time to use your stress management skills. Although trying to imagine a stressful situation will not produce the same intensity as the original stressor, this exercise often gives you a good clue about your specific reactions. Pay attention to these signals rather than ignore them. They will enable you to react when stress is just beginning to build and is more manageable. If you did not notice any reaction, try the exercise again in about a week after you have had some practice using your personal stress gauge.

You now have the basic steps needed to increase your **self-awareness** of stress and keep yourself on a gauge system. With practice this step will take only seconds to complete.

Remember:

- Tune into your stress rather than ignore it.
- Rate your stress level as often as is practical.
- Pay attention to what **your body is telling you.**
- Use the *early warning signals* to your advantage.
- Use the optional biofeedback card to reinforce your self-awareness.

We can now move on to the next skill - **relaxation** - that will help you reduce your stress when it gets beyond your effective stress zone.

# CHAPTER 4

## *Basic Skill Number Two: Relaxation Methods to Quiet the Body*

Being able to relax your body quickly and efficiently is extremely important in our stress management system. Recall that a major part of our stress reaction includes a state of physiological arousal called the *fight-or-flight* response. Relaxation methods can be used to counteract the physical arousal whenever it becomes uncomfortable or pushes us beyond our effective stress zone. This is because relaxation and high physiological arousal are *incompatible* conditions. Since you cannot experience these two conditions at the same time, you will have a considerable advantage in controlling stress as you become better skilled at relaxing your body.

There are literally dozens of relaxation methods you could learn. Perhaps you have already tried some of the methods such as transcendental meditation (TM), self-hypnosis, mindfulness training, biofeedback, or various forms of yoga. Although these and many other methods are quite helpful, our focus here is to help you develop some quick relaxation strategies that work well within a short time framework.

Fortunately, research has found that some common elements are shared among most relaxation methods. Dr. Herbert Benson (1975) of Harvard Medical School conducted very important research to identify these major elements. He found that if certain procedures were followed, the body would automatically relax. Benson refers to this as the ***relaxation response***, which appears to be physically the opposite of the biological stress reaction. Initially, you will need to devote some extra time to practice this method since it takes about 15 - 20 minutes to complete. I have modified the procedure so that after you have had some practice with it, you will be able to use this experience to relax within a minute or two. However, even after you feel confident and skilled at relaxing quickly, you will need to continue with the lengthier procedure to reinforce your skills and also to help prevent some stress related disorders.

## BASIC STEPS TO RELAXATION

After you have read the following material and have a good idea of the basic procedures, test it out. Set aside about 15 - 20 minutes of quiet time when you can try this relaxation method. As with any other skill you learn, do not set yourself up for failure by expecting too much of any method, especially when you are first using it. Relaxation skills take some time to master and as with most things, you will only get better with practice. The full relaxation exercises are most beneficial if you practice daily. Our modified relaxation procedure is as follows:

Find a quiet place where you will not be interrupted.
   1.  Get into a comfortable position, sitting or lying down. It is ideal if you can have all of your body, especially your head, fully

supported. You can use a recliner type chair, or simply lie down in bed or on the floor.

2.  Try to loosen your muscles as best as you can. Briefly pay attention to the tension throughout your body, scanning from your head all the way down to your feet.

3.   Make a mental note of your stress level by rating it from **1** (very relaxed) to **10** (very stressed).

4.   Take a very deep breath through your nose. Breathe in deeply enough to extend your stomach and hold it for a count of four or five seconds. Then breathe out slowly through your mouth. Repeat this three more times.

> Now close your eyes and try to keep all other thoughts out of your mind. Allow your breathing to get into a natural and comfortable pace. Continue to breathe in through your nose and out through your mouth.

> In order to allow the deeper feelings of relaxation to occur, try to find something on which you can focus. Try both of the following methods at different practice times.

> a) Every time you exhale simply say a **word** such as "cope" or "calm" to yourself, and imagine tension flowing out of your body. Focus on your **word** as you breathe naturally.

> b) The next method is particularly good for those who can "visualize" or see things clearly in their mind with their eyes closed. Instead of focusing on a word, imagine a very peaceful and calm **scene**. This can be an imaginary scene or a place you actually recall. These are some popular scenes. Try one of these, or one of your own.

> > Visualize a sunset scene at the beach. Picture the sun slowly setting into the ocean. Feel the warmth of the sun. Focus on the colors and the shape of the sun and clouds.

33

Visualize yourself lying in a forest on a bed of soft pine needles looking up at the sky through the leaves of the trees. Notice the smell of the forest. Focus on a leaf that is falling to the ground in slow motion.

Visualize a pleasant place from your past (a park, backyard, favorite fishing spot, etc.).

5. Continue breathing naturally and focusing on your **word** or your **scene**. Do not be concerned if you get distracted. Try to bring yourself back to the procedure and continue focusing for about 15-20 minutes.

6. When you finish, sit quietly for a few minutes and make a mental note of your stress level (rating it from **1** to **10**). Notice any sensations you experience such as warmth, heaviness, or tingling sensations. These are good signs of relaxation.

7. Open your eyes, but do not stand up suddenly. Remain *calm* in your body, but *alert* in your mind. When you feel alert and ready to get up, do so, but try to **remember** the calm relaxed feelings and sensations you have just experienced.

For the first two weeks it will help if you record a "before" and "after" stress rating when you practice these methods. A graph for recording two weeks of your stress ratings is included at the end of the chapter. Make a copy of the graph to see progress in reducing your stress with our procedures. For audio recordings of various relaxation methods, you can also go to the **http://www.icope.co** site.

If you have any problems with this type of procedure, which is a more passive form of relaxation, experiment with it to make it work for you on a more personal level. Try different locations, different images, or even different times of the day to practice the exercises. You may also want to substitute some "soothing" music to focus on rather than a visual image for your relaxation exercises. If you are an energetic person, you may find the procedure particularly difficult. If so, you may want to try other procedures such as more physical forms of releasing tension. Exercising, taking a walk, riding a bike, etc. may be more helpful for you to relax.

## BEYOND BASIC RELAXATION METHODS

You might be asking yourself, "How can I use these methods in everyday situations?" Obviously, you cannot lie down for 15-20 minutes every time you feel stressed. However, what you can do is get in the habit of practicing the **deep breathing portion** of the procedure every time you notice a significant level of stress. As is summarized on the optional biofeedback card, taking two deep breaths and holding them for about 4-5 seconds will help you feel more relaxed. You will not get as deeply relaxed as you would with the complete procedure, but during most day-to-day situations you will not be trying to produce deep states of relaxation. Many people find that a few deep breaths in combination with the rest of the iCope strategies will be sufficient to return them to their effective stress zone. This is particularly helpful for sudden increases in your stress level or when you are preparing to confront a stressful situation. For example, if you are about to go into an important exam or meeting, make a difficult phone call, stand up before a class to give a speech, or go into a frightening place, you will probably want to use the relaxation methods *prior* to encountering the situation. This will help you cope with those anticipated stressors more effectively.

If you are having problems associated with more chronic stress (e.g., headaches, high blood pressure, insomnia, etc.) it will be helpful if you continue using the full relaxation methods described earlier, or try the optional audio recordings on the **iCope.co** website. These more sustained efforts at physical relaxation in addition to the other iCope strategies in your day-to-day situations will be beneficial for chronic stress.

For relaxation methods to be an effective coping method in various settings, remember:

- Relaxation is a skill that will take time and practice to master.
- Initially use the full relaxation method at home on a daily basis.
- While practicing the full procedure, pair deep breathing with your deeply relaxed state.
- Begin to take two deep breaths frequently throughout your daily routines, especially when you are stressed.
- Continue to use the full relaxation methods as needed to reinforce your skills.

Now that we have a basic strategy to quiet the body, let's move on to strategies that can help quiet the mind.

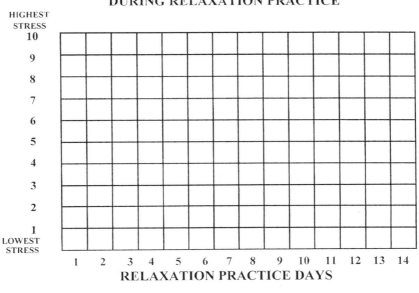

GRAPH OF STRESS RATINGS (1-10)
DURING RELAXATION PRACTICE

FOR PRE-RELAXATION RATINGS, connect ratings with a dashed ----------- line.

FOR POST-RELAXATION RATINGS, connect ratings with a solid _____ line.

Figure 4-1. Chart your progress in practicing the relaxation method by recording each pre- and post-relaxation stress rating. Put a data point in the appropriate box for each practice session. After a few days of practice, connect the pre-relaxation scores with a dashed line and the post-relaxation scores with a solid line. This will give you visual feedback about the effectiveness of the relaxation method in reducing your stress scores.

# CHAPTER 5

## *Basic Skill Number Three: Talking Rationally to Yourself*

Imagine yourself at school. You just returned from your lunch period and your teacher gives you a note from the principal or dean. This is unusual since you have never received a note like this. The note simply says: "I will be back in my office at 2:30 this afternoon and need to meet with you promptly at 3:00 PM to discuss something important. See you this afternoon." What thoughts would go through your mind when processing this note? Try to list three thoughts here or on a separate piece of paper:

1._____

2._____

3._____

Would this note about a meeting be a stressor for you? If so, do your thoughts about the note add to your stress? Obviously, each person will have some unique thoughts in processing this kind of event. Interestingly, the majority of us in our culture would respond with initial negative thoughts such as:

*What did I do now?*
*Did I forget to do something?*
*Someone must be upset with me.*
*Is there a problem at home?*
*I can't get in trouble now!*

Thoughts like these are likely to magnify the stressor and our total stress reaction will intensify. We could just as easily have had other thoughts that would have been less negative, such as:

*I wonder if I'm getting that award I wanted.*
*They probably need some standard information.*
*I wish I had more information about this meeting, but I don't have anything to worry about.*

As was discussed in the introductory chapter, we mentally process all of our stressors like a computer. This processing often seems automatic and unconscious at times. Unfortunately, many of us have been conditioned to process events in a relatively negative way that intensifies our stress. What could be neutral becomes worrisome and stressful. What typically would create some distress now creates a much more intense reaction.

Certain beliefs or values that we have learned in our culture from our parents, teachers, peers, and religious authorities, act as magnifiers of stress in just about all of us. Fortunately, we can change how we look at and interpret situations so that we do not overreact to stressful situations. Rather than magnify our stress, we can learn to **filter** out some of its impact on us.

As is true with other aspects of stress management, we must first become more aware of our beliefs, attitudes, and the mental processes that take place in response to stress. Dr. Albert Ellis and several colleagues such as Maxie Maultsby (1984) and Robert Harper (Ellis & Harper, 1975) pioneered much of this work in understanding how our cognitive (*mental*) processes operate in creating and controlling emotional distress.

## FOUR MENTAL HABITS THAT INTENSIFY STRESS

In order to become more sensitive to how mental processes can contribute to your own stress, ask yourself if you fall into any of these common traps:

1. Do you tend to **catastrophize** or make things seem dramatically worse than they really are? If so, you are often likely to see situations deteriorating or leading to tragic conclusions. You probably tend to exaggerate and blow things out of proportion. If you catastrophize, you will have a lot more "drama" in your life.

2. Do you tend to **see things in absolute terms**? In other words, do you think in an **all or none** fashion? If so, you would see things in black and white and have a hard time seeing the gray in between. This would lead you to "**over-generalize**" in response to certain events and your language will reflect this. Words like *never, always, everyone, no one*, and *impossible* are often voiced by those who are thought of as "black-and-white" thinkers.

3. Do you have **excessive expectations** of yourself and/or others? If so, thoughts such as "I must" or "you should" probably will run

through your mind and your vocabulary. Since these expectations are not realistic, you are likely to be disappointed in yourself as well as others. Depending on how you handle this, you might find yourself very angry or depressed.

4. Do you **focus on the negative** and tend to ignore the positive? If this is true for you, you may operate as if you have tunnel vision and your attention is likely to focus on what is *wrong, bad, terrible*, etc. You can easily spot flaws in people, places and things. Your negative attitude may set you up to complain about most things, to be dissatisfied, and to get angry or depressed easily, all of which could lead to social problems as well.

These are four of the most common mental processes that create much of our distress. These processes are like any other habits in that they are hard to break unless we are highly motivated to change them. However, even when we want to change these **mental habits**, we still need a good approach in order to be successful. These methods will be presented later in the book.

## BELIEFS THAT CAUSE STRESS

In addition to learning what some of your **mental habits** are, you want to increase your awareness of whether you are magnifying your stressors by examining your **specific beliefs** and attitudes. We are all likely to have some strong beliefs that cause extra distress. Complete Exercise 5-1 below which will help identify some of your troublesome beliefs.

Exercise 5-1. Rate how true or false each of these beliefs is for you.

|  | Mostly False | Somewhat True | Mostly True |
|---|---|---|---|
| 1. I must have *love and approval* of almost everyone who is important to me. |  |  |  |
| 2. I must be *thoroughly competent* at most things I do. |  |  |  |
| 3. The *world should be fair* and others who treat me unfairly should be punished. |  |  |  |
| 4. My emotions are controlled by external events and there's *little I can do about my emotional state.* |  |  |  |
| 5. I need to *worry about bad or dangerous things* that might happen. |  |  |  |
| 6. I need to have *someone* on whom I can depend and who *should take care of me.* |  |  |  |
| 7. There is *one correct/perfect solution to every problem* and it should be found. |  |  |  |

## COMPLETE EXERCISE 5-1 BEFORE READING ON

Look over your answers and note which items were *Somewhat True* and especially those that were *Mostly True*. These are some of the beliefs that have been described by Ellis and his colleagues as being essentially **irrational**. As such, they can be major culprits in causing more stress than you need to experience. It should be noted that these just happen to be some of the most common beliefs in our culture that increase stress. Other irrational beliefs can include thoughts such as: "My past must continue to affect me and I cannot change how I feel or react," or "I cannot stop from being upset over the problems of other people." Each of us can also have our own individual beliefs that also magnify our reaction to certain events. All of these irrational beliefs serve as magnifiers of stress, and it would be to your benefit to modify those beliefs. Fortunately, this can be done by learning how to challenge and to re-frame irrational beliefs. By doing this **cognitive restructuring**, you can diffuse much of the unwanted stress you encounter.

If you exhibit any of the four troublesome *mental habits* (**catastrophizing, overgeneralizing, expecting too much,** or **focusing on the negative**), or strongly hold on to any of the major *irrational beliefs*, you will want to use the following psychological strategy to diffuse your stress reactions. If you continue to practice these methods of **rational self-talk** or **cognitive restructuring**, they can be a powerful coping skill that will be extremely helpful in managing your stress.

## PROBLEMS ASSOCIATED WITH IRRATIONAL BELIEFS

*In addition to magnifying our stress reactions, additional problems can be caused by strongly holding on to the different beliefs. Following are a few examples of some potential problems associated with irrational beliefs.*

| Having this belief: | Leads to: |
|---|---|
| I must have love/approval. | Insecurity. Social anxiety due to the fear of rejection. Avoiding social contacts. Being a "yes man". Passive behavior. |
| I must be thoroughly competent. | Perfectionism. Depression because 100% success is impossible. Overly critical of self and others. |
| I expect "fairness" and blame others including parents for unfair treatment. | Vindictive behavior. Self-righteous approach to dealing with others. Non-compliance with authority figures. |
| I have little control over my emotions. | Helplessness. Failure to eliminate magnifiers. |
| I need to worry about fearful or dangerous things. | Excessive fears. Avoidance of reasonable risks. Obsessing about the future. |
| I need others to take care of me. | Excessive dependency. Anger when others "let you down." |
| There is one correct solution to my problem (or one way to do things). | Rigid, controlling, or obsessive-compulsive personality. |
| Fill in: *My personal irrational belief:* | Fill in: *The effects this has on me:* |

## YOUR NEW LANGUAGE

Now that you are more sensitive to the fact that your mental habits and beliefs about a stressful event can magnify your reaction, you can begin to diffuse any irrational or negative thinking. These types of thinking patterns are probably going on throughout your daily activities. Since they are likely to be somewhat automatic and unconscious, you can become more aware of them by asking yourself some questions whenever your stress level changes. For example, when an event occurs that increases your stress noticeably, ask yourself what you are thinking about the situation. What am I telling myself? Is this stressor triggering any of my irrational beliefs? Are some of my stress-producing mental habits, such as catastrophizing or overgeneralizing, kicking in?

46

The **Stress Analysis Chart** at the end of the chapter can help you become more aware of your stress producing self-talk, which in turn will allow you change it. You can download a blank copy of the form at **http://www.icope.co** and make several copies of the chart for your use. Whenever you notice a significant stress reaction, record your thoughts and your reaction in the left column. As you get in the habit of noticing any of your irrational or negative thinking, you will begin to learn a new language. This language produces less stress by keeping things in perspective - it keeps us more rational. This new language is represented on the right hand column of the chart. Here, thoughts and statements about the stressful event are likely to be more rational and positive. Many of these statements directly challenge and dispute any irrational thoughts that were identified.

Using these cognitive methods does not mean that tragic, painful, or upsetting situations will feel good. However, what it does mean is that *the event will not be made any more stressful than it has to be*. Your stress might still be elevated, but your new way of thinking can reduce the stress level and keep the emotional reaction to a minimum. Instead of feeling so angry and outraged about an event that you are ready to react violently, you might instead feel frustration and resentment. Rather than getting seriously depressed, you might feel only saddened by the situation. Keeping things in perspective can help keep your anxiety under control rather than having it escalate to a *panic attack*.

Examples of some old and new ways of thinking are shown on completed Stress Analysis Charts at the end of the chapter. Use this process on a regular basis to see how well you can translate your thoughts into more rational statements.

The key here is learning a new way of thinking - essentially learning a new language. Our old language that magnifies our stress can be so strong that it will take a lot of patience and practice to learn the new language. Just as if you were learning a foreign language, you would go through stages where the translation process is awkward and cumbersome. You have to consciously think of the correct way to say something and then translate from one language to the other. This is also true with learning how to talk rationally to yourself. Over time, you will begin to speak fluently if you continue to practice. However, anyone who has taken a foreign language in school will recall that when it is not used regularly, we can barely remember that language. This will also happen with the language of **rational self-talk**. You will need to use it regularly in order to be successful in developing your coping skills. Do not get discouraged if you still catch yourself slipping back into negative stress-inducing self-talk. It could take months to integrate rational self-talk fully into your life.

## REVIEW TIME

Here are a few general reminders about learning to talk rationally to yourself. Take a few seconds to think as rationally and positively as possible whenever you are stressed. Ask and tell yourself:

- *What is making me so stressed?*
- *It is probably not as bad as I think.*
- *I've handled situations like this before.*
- *I can calm myself and feel better later.*
- *My goal is to minimize my stress reaction.*

If these thoughts and the rest of the iCope strategy are not controlling your stress effectively, practice the disputing and challenging skills that you used on the Stress Analysis Chart. Make your statements **specific to the exact stressor you are facing**. Again, the goal is to keep things in perspective so that your stress is not exaggerated unnecessarily. Remember you are still going to feel some emotional reaction, especially if this is a significant event. Do not try to lie to yourself because this will not work.  For example, if you feel distressed about a situation, telling yourself that you **do not care** about it will **not** make you feel better.

With regular practice it is reasonable that you will become proficient in these skills. Over time you will begin to encounter a wider range of stressful events that you can reinterpret with your rational language. Like any other skill, the more successful you are in controlling your stress, the easier and more quickly you will be able to use these methods.

You now have the major techniques for **mentally** or **psychologically** controlling your stress. In addition to maintaining your other skills (self-awareness and relaxing physically), remember the general principles of the **cognitive methods** covered in this chapter:

- Talk calmly to yourself when a stressor occurs.
- Try to keep the stressful event in perspective.
- Reassure yourself of your abilities to *manage* the stress.
- Avoid *catastrophizing, overgeneralizing, maintaining unreasonable expectations*, and *focusing on the negative*.
- Use your *rational self-talk* to reinterpret and challenge any irrational beliefs.

The three main strategies discussed thus far (**self-awareness**, **physical relaxation**, and the **cognitive/psychological strategies**) focus on controlling your stress reactions. Now we can move on to methods that give you more control over the actual stressful events.

## *STRESS ANALYSIS CHART*

**STRESSFUL EVENT:**

_____

_____

_____

| Old Way of Thinking *(Magnifying the Stressor)* **IRRATIONAL SELF-TALK** | New Way of Thinking *(Filtering the Stressor)* **RATIONAL SELF-TALK** |
|---|---|
| 1. _____ | 1. _____ |
| 2. _____ | 2. _____ |
| 3. _____ | 3. _____ |
| 4. _____ | 4. _____ |
| 5. _____ | 5. _____ |
| **OLD STRESS REACTION:** | **CONTROLLED REACTION:** |
| Physiological: _____ | Physiological: _____ |
| Emotional: _____ | Emotional: _____ |
| Mental: _____ | Mental: _____ |
| Behavioral: _____ | Behavioral: _____ |
| **STRESS LEVEL (1-10):_____** | **STRESS LEVEL (1-10):_____** |

# *STRESS ANALYSIS CHART* (SAMPLE 1)

### STRESSFUL EVENT: *I lost my wallet today*

Old Way of Thinking:
*(Magnifying the Stressor)*
**IRRATIONAL SELF TALK**

New Way of Thinking:
*(Filtering the Stressor)*
**RATIONAL SELF TALK:**

**1.** *How stupid can I be?*

1. *Everyone makes mistakes - this has nothing to do with intelligence.*

**2.** *This is the worst thing that could happen to me.*

2. *This is definitely a problem, but it's not the worst thing that could happen to me.*

**3.** *Everyone will be angry with me.*

3. *My mother or father might be upset, but I can cope with their reactions. I will take responsibility for this.*

**4.** *There is no way I can fix this.*

4. *It might take time, but I can get everything except cash in my wallet replaced.*

### OLD STRESS REACTION:

**Physiological:** *upset stomach*

**Emotional:** *angry, frustrated*

**Mental:** *worried*

**Behavioral**: *avoid going home*

### CONTROLLED REACTION:

**Physiological:** *calm*

**Emotional:** *less upset*

**Mental:** *thinking of a plan*

**Behavioral:** *call home to let them know I lost my wallet and that I will be home soon*

**STRESS LEVEL (1-10): 8**

**STRESS LEVEL (1-10): 6**

51

# *STRESS ANALYSIS CHART* (SAMPLE 2)

**STRESSFUL EVENT:** *My job is being eliminated with no good explanation. I was fired!*

| **IRRATIONAL SELF TALK** *(Magnifying the Stressor)* | **RATIONAL SELF TALK:** *(Filtering the Stressor)* |
|---|---|
| 1. *I am a failure. If I were perfect, this would not have happened.* | 1. *There are reasons for this happening - it is not due to a lack of perfection. If I made mistakes, I will correct them in the future.* |
| 2. *I'll never find another good job.* | 2. *It may take time, but there is no reason that I will not be able able to find a good job. I can do this.* |
| 3. *Everyone will be disappointed in me.* | 3. *Some, not all, people will be disappointed about my job loss - not me. I can accept that since I cannot keep everyone happy.* |
| 4. *My company has no right to do this to me. It's not fair.* | 4. *Unfortunately they can do this. They hired me and legally they can fire me. I do not like it, but fairness has nothing to do with this.* |

| **OLD STRESS REACTION:** | **CONTROLLED REACTION:** |
|---|---|
| Physiological: *tightness in my chest* | Physiological: *no physical distress* |
| Emotional: *angry* | Emotional: *disappointed* |
| Mental: *questioning my skills* | Mental: *reassuring myself about what I can do to find a good job* |
| Behavioral: *pacing in my room* | Behavioral: *lying down, relaxing with music* |
| STRESS LEVEL (1-10): 8 | STRESS LEVEL (1-10): 5 |

# CHAPTER **6**

# *Basic Skill Number Four:*
# *Problem Solving*

By this time you have had practice at ***increasing your awareness*** of your stress level, ***relaxing your body*** when you are under stress, and ***talking rationally to yourself*** in order to keep things in perspective. These three skills provide you with your initial defense in dealing with the daily stressors that occur. Even when you are coping well using these methods, many stressors still require further action in order to deal with them more effectively. Whenever a stressor requires more extensive and deliberate action on your part, it is safe to assume that the stressor has now become a **problem**. In reality, many stressors are on-going problems.

Keeping in mind that a "problem" is any stressful situation that requires some deliberate action on your part, look at the following list of events and think about those that you would classify as problems.

1. Running out of gas on the highway.
2. Getting a bad final grade in one of your classes.
3. Being attracted to someone you don't know at a party.
4. Having a relationship end.

5. Getting caught using alcohol/drugs by your parents.
6. Transferring to a new school.
7. Not having a good social group of friends.
8. Losing your keys or wallet.
9. Finding out that you or a family member has a serious illness.
10. Having to give an oral presentation in class.

As you probably guessed, all of these would be considered problems. Clearly, they can range from relatively minor events, such as not finding your keys, to potentially serious events such as an illness. Recognizing that many stressful events can be viewed as problems can help you handle the situation more effectively. First, some problems can be resolved successfully and you will feel relieved from the stress. For example, finding your lost keys or wallet, or having someone bring you gas for your car will lead to a fairly quick reduction in stress. Another reason it helps to look at stressors as problems is that **every problem has certain options or alternatives that can help alleviate (though not necessarily eliminate) the stress caused by the problem**. This is especially relevant for more serious problems. Finally, reminding yourself that this situation is *simply* a problem that requires some action will help you keep the problem in perspective and deal with the challenge of coping with it. Having confidence that you can and will use effective problem solving abilities will be helpful in managing your stress. Before we get into **problem solving** strategies, we first need to dispel some myths about problems.

**Myth #1. *There is a perfect solution for any significant problem*.** If you tend to believe this, you will probably be very frustrated with how you handle some problems. You might also set yourself up for disappointment or even a sense of failure. There usually are no perfect solutions for big problems. Certainly, some alternatives will be better and more effective than others. The goal of problem solving is to find the alternatives that help you cope most effectively with the situation. The sooner you accept that there will not be one perfect solution available, the easier your problem solving will be.

**Myth #2.** *Sometimes there are problems for which there are no alternatives to help cope with the situation.* It is true that some problems are "unsolvable" in the sense that the actual events can never be changed (such as the death of a loved one or having your parents divorce), but there are always options to better cope with the problem. *We need to avoid telling ourselves that nothing can be done to deal with a particular problem.* There are always alternatives and we can learn to be more creative in identifying and selecting positive strategies. The eventual goal with some problems is not to undo the event, but instead to develop an "active coping style" where you automatically begin to process your options when confronted with the problem. Try to avoid a "passive coping style" which revolves around waiting for things to happen rather than making things happen. Passivity sets you up to believe you have no control or choices. This can lead to feelings of helplessness, which is truly an unhealthy emotion.

**Myth #3.** *We must be 100% certain which options are best before deciding how we want to approach the problem.* This belief leads to considerable indecisiveness because we are seldom 100% sure of any decision. We often feel some ambivalence or uncertainty regarding the choices we make. One aspect of good problem solving is the ability to accept whatever level of ambivalence or risk that accompanies our decisions. If an error is made, we can simply go back and reevaluate the situation and make new choices.

**Myth #4.** *The faster you solve a problem, the better the outcome.* It is likely that responding too quickly or impulsively will not be very effective. This is in direct contrast to the desire for 100% certainty. Usually there is a middle ground where you take enough time to process your alternatives, but not so much time that you end up avoiding any final decision about how to deal with your problem. If you tend to be impulsive, you will want to slow yourself down a bit. You can still be a "decisive" person without being impulsive.

## BASIC STEPS IN PROBLEM SOLVING

The five basic steps to creative problem solving are rather easy to learn. Many of us have already learned our own way of handling difficult life experiences with the help of parents, friends, teachers, or spiritual leaders. However, like other stress management skills, it takes practice with many different types of problems to become proficient enough for the procedures to become more automatic. As older teens or young adults, you may have others, especially parents, who might try to do much of your problem solving and decision-making. Sometimes this works well when not overdone, but at other times you may want more control in handling your own problems. With maturity and more independence, you will want to incorporate their input with your own skills. Using the steps in this chapter may help you find the right balance of counting on input from others and managing problems on your own.

As we describe the steps in problem solving, you are likely to see some things that you already do and other things that you are not doing. If you need improvement in problem solving, try to follow all of the steps. In the beginning it is best to actually write down your options. Later, you can process most situations mentally without writing down all the details.

Although you can learn to process many problems within a reasonable period of time, it will take longer to evaluate significant problems that are more difficult to handle. It would be wise to get others such as trusted friends, mentors, or parents involved in generating options when you are faced with very tough problems.

56

The basic steps in problem solving are:

1. Define the problem as specifically as you can.
2. List several alternatives to help you solve the problem or at least cope with the problem.
3. Think of the positives and negatives of each option.
4. Select the best *combination* of options to develop an active plan for dealing with the situation.
5. Put the plan of action into effect and evaluate its outcome.

**Step #1. Define each problem as specifically as you can and focus on one problem at a time.**

The following is a poorly defined problem:
*"I'm really upset with my best friend."*

A slightly better defined problem might be:
*"My friend often does things that aggravate me."*

An even more specific problem could be defined as:
*"This is the second time this month that my friend cancelled our weekend plans at the last minute."*

Your friend in this example might very well do many things that are aggravating. He might be very irresponsible in general and create many problems on a day-to-day basis. How you approach this situation will depend on how you define the problem. If you are trying to come up with appropriate alternatives for the friend's "general irresponsibility" as opposed to the immediate need to deal with your frustration and disappointment, you will most likely come up with *different* options to deal with the two *different* problems.

## Step #2. List several alternatives to help cope with the problem.

Whenever you confront a problem, begin to think of alternatives that could be implemented. **Avoid at all costs the thought that *"nothing can be done."*** Be as creative as possible in generating your ideas. Often we have a tendency to rule out options before we have fully analyzed the problem. Again, try not to do this. If you think of an alternative, write it down and fully evaluate it later.

Try to think of at least three alternatives for coping with a new problem with your "irresponsible" friend. The new problem is that you loaned your friend one of your expensive textbooks from school and he has lost the book. Below is a list of options generated by a small group that brainstormed the problem. Look it over and you are likely to see options that seem *unacceptable* to you. However, this type of creativity is what you would want to generate in your problem solving efforts. You want to have a wide range of options that you can rule out *later*. If you do not generate alternatives that later seem *unacceptable* to you, it is likely that you are not being as creative as possible.

1. Text your friend that you need the money to replace the book immediately.
2. Text or tell your friend that you want to get together very soon to discuss the book situation.
3. Let your friend know that you will not be loaning him anything in the future.
4. Call your friend's parents and ask that they refund you the cost of the book.
5. Ask your friend what he is doing to find or replace the book.
6. Let your friend know that the situation is very upsetting to you and ask that he find a way to correct these types of conflicts in the future.
7. End your friendship since it's just too much work to maintain.

## Step #3. Rate each of your alternatives.

Look at each of your options and think of its pros and cons. This will help you select the more positive alternatives and enable you to design an effective action plan. Initially, you might want to rate each alternative on a four-point rating system on the work sheet. This is a little more time consuming now, but will help you with future problem solving efforts when you are not using the work sheets.

## Step #4. Select the best alternatives to design an active plan to cope with the problem.

Sometimes one alternative is sufficient to deal with the situation effectively. However, it is quite common to combine two or three options to formulate your solution. Be creative in how you put together your better alternatives.

## Step #5.  Put your plan into action as soon as possible.

Your problem solving skills will not be useful unless you follow through by implementing the plan and evaluating its success. Because we are not perfect at this skill, it is expected that some action plans will not be very effective and will require modification. If a plan is not working satisfactorily, go back to your initial step and repeat the process. You may find that the problem was not defined properly or that other alternatives need to be generated. You will also have new information that might change your ratings of the alternatives already generated. By practicing the five steps regularly you are likely to notice that you automatically begin the problem solving process when you encounter new stressors.

Two Problem Solving Worksheet examples are shown below to give you an idea of the basic process. The blank work sheet can be copied and used to record your own problem solving efforts. Using these work sheets is only temporary and eventually you will only want to use them for significant problems. The more routine stressors can typically be handled by mentally processing the relevant information and alternatives.

Serious problems cannot be processed immediately. These situations will require longer periods of deliberate thought about the problem, issues, and the available alternatives. Talking to others to help you formulate a plan is certainly beneficial at these times. However, our basic philosophy emphasizes that even though you cannot change certain events (e.g., death of a loved one, an unwanted end of a relationship, or a physical or psychological trauma), you can generate options that will help you **cope** with those events. This proactive approach to serious problems keeps you psychologically in a healthier frame of mind and helps prevent feelings of helplessness. For problem solving, remember:

- *Focus on the specific problem* being confronted.
- Remind yourself that there are alternatives over which **you have some control**.
- Maintain an active coping style and avoid telling yourself "**nothing can be done**."
- **Avoid impulsive actions, looking for the perfect solution, or 100% certainty**.
- Mentally process your options and **put a plan into action**.
- **Stay flexible**. If your action plan is not successful, reevaluate the situation.

## PROBLEM SOLVING WORKSHEET

**1. Define the problem as specifically as you can.**

**2. List up to five alternatives to help cope with the problem.**

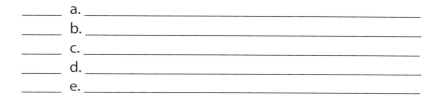

_____    a. _____
_____    b. _____
_____    c. _____
_____    d. _____
_____    e. _____

**3. Go over the alternatives and rate each one with the following 4-point rating scale:**

    4 = Definite positive approach
    3 = Very good possibility (mostly positive)
    2 = Slight possibility (positive but with some concerns)
    1 = Unlikely possibility (too many negatives at this time)

**4. Based on your evaluation of the alternatives, write an action plan to cope with the problem.**

_____
_____
_____
_____

**5. Put the plan into action and evaluate the success of your plan within a specific time framework.** If your action plan is not working satisfactorily, repeat the process with any new information you have (e.g., new alternatives).

**Date to evaluate plan:** _____

## *PROBLEM SOLVING WORKSHEET* (SAMPLE 1)

1.  **Define the problem as specifically as you can.**

    *I received my first SAT scores and I am at least 200 points below what I will need to get into the college I want to attend*

2.  List five alternatives to help cope with the problem.

    1   a. *Apply to my 1ˢᵗ choice colleges & hope for the best.*
    2   b. *Take many practice tests & retake the SAT*
    3   c. *Sign up for a class specializing in SAT prep*
    3   d. *Get a tutor who specializes in the SAT*
    2   e. *Do extra work at school on my weak areas*

3.  **Go over the alternatives and rate each one with the following 4-point summary:**

    **4**   Definite positive approach
    **3**   Very good possibility (mostly positive)
    **2**   Slight possibility (somewhat positive, but some negatives as well)
    **1**   Unlikely possibility (too many negatives at this time; possibly a last resort alternative)

4.  **Based on your evaluation of the alternatives, write out your action plan to cope with the problem.**

    *I will talk with my parents about the money to either get a tutor or sign up for a class to retake the SAT - I will also take one full practice test each weekend until the next SAT exam.*

5.  **Put the plan into action and evaluate the success of your plan within a specific time framework.** If your action plan is not working satisfactorily, repeat the process with any new information you have (e.g., new alternatives).

**Date to evaluate plan:** *In two months when second SAT is done.*

# *PROBLEM SOLVING WORKSHEET* (SAMPLE 2)

1. **Define the problem as specifically as you can.**

   *I lost my friend's expensive camera on a trip -
   I should replace it even though I do not have the money.*

2. List five alternatives to help cope with the problem.

   3     a. *Even though my parents are upset, ask them for a loan*
   3     b. *Get a part-time job on weekends to earn the extra cash*
   2     c. *Sell some of my possessions for cash to repay my friend*
   1     d. *Tell my friend I'm sorry but I can't pay for the camera*
   3     e. *Ask my friend if I can pay for this over time*

3. **Go over the alternatives and rate each one with the following
   4-point summary**:

   4        Definite positive approach
   3        Very good possibility (mostly positive)
   2        Slight possibility (somewhat positive, but some negatives as well)
   1        Unlikely possibility (too many negatives at this time; possibly a last
   resort alternative)

4. **Based on your evaluation of the alternatives, write out your action plan to cope
   with the problem.**

   *I will borrow part of the money from my parents to give
   to my friend and ask if I can repay the rest over the
   next 4 months. I will get a part-time job or sell some things over
   the next 4 months to repay my friend the full amount.*

5. **Put the plan into action and evaluate the success of your plan within a specific
   time framework.** If your action plan is not working satisfactorily, repeat the process
   with any new information you have (e.g., new alternatives).

**Date to evaluate plan: In** *2 months so, I have time to revise this if I do not
think I will have enough money in 4 months to fully pay for*    *the
camera.*

63

# CHAPTER 7

## *Improving Resilience to Stress*

By now you have learned the four basic iCope strategies of stress management. A summary of the steps is presented at the end of this chapter. Four things will help improve your success in mastering this approach to coping with stress. First, you will need to **practice** the core skills: **self-awareness**, **relaxation**, **talking rationally to yourself**, and **problem solving**. With regular practice you will be able use these methods to cope more effectively with many of the routine stressors that occur on a daily basis.

Second, it is important to **remain flexible** in your attempts at controlling stress. At times, each of us needs to adjust our approach to meet our specific needs. Maintain your willingness to revise strategies to see what works best for you. Reading other materials in the reference section will also give you more variety and greater depth on the key strategies described in this book.

The third way to improve your chances for success is to **keep your expectations realistic**. Remember, it will take time to become skilled at these methods. It is also important to remind yourself that you cannot eliminate stress. Keep everything in perspective. In your early attempts at using the iCope methods, look for small improvements in your ability to manage stress.

Finally, as was mentioned earlier in the book, each of us needs to **use a variety of methods to cope** with all the different types of stressors that we face. Therefore, it is important to recognize that there will be times when the strategies in this book alone will not be sufficient. Although the basic skills are likely to be helpful with general stress, major life events will require some additional methods. At these times, try to be as creative as possible in your problem solving skills to consider all of your options. Many stressful situations involve conflicts with others, excessive time demands, or significant changes in your life. Additional strategies can be found in Supplements A (assertiveness and anger management), B (time management & organizational skills), C (self-esteem and confidence), and D (major life events), as well as in the recommended readings.

## RESILIENCE AND VULNERABILITY TO STRESS

An important issue to discuss is your general **resilience**, or its counter-part, **vulnerability**, to stress. Various assessment devices have been used over the years to test vulnerability to stress. Factors that indicate higher resilience (i.e., low vulnerability) include your skills and positive habits, social supports, good physical condition and sense of well-being, assertiveness, and avoidance of ineffective coping methods such as using alcohol or cigarettes. Other resources available to you – such as family, friends, and a spiritual connection of some sort – can also increase your resilience.  If your resilience to stress is relatively high, you will be better prepared to deal with the various stressors that could impact upon you at any time. In contrast, high vulnerability to stress suggests that you are more susceptible to the negative effects of stress. If you fall into this latter category, it would be in your best interest to take some steps soon to increase your resilience, thereby reducing your overall vulnerability.

The **healthy habits** that will help your physical stamina better tolerate stress include:

- eating at least one well-balanced meal per day;
- getting adequate sleep most days of the week (6-8 hours);
- having physical exertion/exercise a few times per week;
- maintaining your weight at a healthy level; and
- avoiding excessive consumption of caffeine, alcohol, and cigarettes.

Some **social factors** related to confidence and self-esteem will also help increase your resilience. This includes maintaining your network of friends, having at least one or more *close* friends or family members to confide in regarding personal issues, and being able to discuss problems and express feelings with those who are closest to you. We should all have at least one close friend that can be called in an emergency at 3:00 AM!

Finally, there are some **lifestyle patterns** that can also reduce your vulnerability to stress. Maintain balance in your life with time to enjoy fun/leisure activities while you meet your normal responsibilities at school, at work, and at home. Try to attend important social events and to have some quiet time for yourself, even if it's only a little time, to relax and defuse from your daily hassles and pressures.

After you become successful in using the basic methods in this book to cope with day-to-day stressors, you will benefit from taking some preventive steps to reduce your overall vulnerability to stress. By making some of these changes in your lifestyle you can improve your resistance to many stress related problems. Strong evidence suggests that our *immune system* is very sensitive to stress. An oversimplified interpretation of the research is that our immune system is weakened under chronic stress to the point that we could actually become more susceptible to many diseases. Preliminary research findings indicate that learning how to cope actively with stress (rather than passively ignoring or accepting all the stress that you encounter) can actually reduce your risk for serious illness. Many universities and medical centers around the country now include some form of coping skills training as an adjunct to their standard medical care for many serious medical problems. The preventive methods described below are all *proactive* ways of coping.

---

### STRESS AND THE IMMUNE SYSTEM

*The importance of managing stress should be very apparent by now. However, it is important to discuss the potentially dangerous situation that can arise if you let stress become a chronic problem. Researchers have known for many decades that chronic stress can cause serious physiological problems such as high blood pressure, ulcers, and headache pain. In more recent years, the evidence has been mounting that stress also causes damage at the cellular level. One interesting finding is that in addition to genetic factors, significant stress can contribute to gray hair. Although there is no suggestion that a traumatic event will cause gray hair overnight, there is evidence that the cells that produce melanin, which gives hair its color, are damaged by stress. As these cells die off, as they normally do with age, the hair does not have enough melanin to give it color. Stress appears to speed up the aging process of these cells to produce a visible sign of the damage.*

---

*The impact of stress on hair color is interesting (at least to older adults). However, the more serious threat of stress on our health might provide us with more motivation to handle stress in proactive ways. As mentioned earlier, chronic stress can have an adverse effect on our immune system. Since our immune system is our primary defense against everything from the common cold to cancer cells, it is important to be aware of your risks if your immune system is compromised. Although* **short-term stress** *can activate your immune system in a positive way,* **long-term stress***, which will produce too much cortisol and other stress hormones, will be detrimental. The process is briefly summarized below.*

*We all have certain cells that the immune system uses to protect us by attacking virus-infected cells, mutant cells, and transplanted tissue. Two of the types of cells that get a lot of research attention are T-cells and Natural Killer (NK) cells. Much of the research with both animals and humans shows that significant stress with its high cortisol levels will prevent T-cells from maturing and will also decrease NK cell counts. This could be harmful for anyone who has a compromised immune system (e.g., HIV+ individuals or those receiving chemotherapy). Fortunately, considerable research indicates that relaxation methods, rational self-talk, exercise, a good social support network, and proactive stress management skills can all increase T-cell and NK cell counts as well as other biochemical improvements to the immune system.*

## PREVENTIVE MEASURES

When it comes to evaluating the importance of our vulnerability to stress and its related diseases, the message from an old famous oil filter commercial is apropos. The commercial, pointing out the value of doing something relatively minor now in order to prevent major costly engine repairs later, would usually end with a tag line something like: *"You can pay me now, or pay me later."* This same message is relevant to stress management. You can spend some time and effort now learning to cope more actively with stress, or you can let things go until the complications are more severe, such as headaches, ulcers, high blood pressure, or even life-threatening illnesses. Research continues to support the finding that people who are *active copers* have better physical resilience to certain illnesses. *Active copers* are those who try to take control of various aspects of their lives to confront issues and problems. Those who tend to give up or see themselves as "helpless" may be more susceptible to any medical problems that are worsened by stress.

Obviously, it is highly recommended that you take some action now to improve your resilience. In addition to maintaining the four core iCope strategies, the 10 major preventive steps that are likely to decrease your vulnerability to stress are listed below.

1.  Develop a regular program for relaxing.

2.  Develop outside interests for recreation and leisure time.

3.  Develop a healthy lifestyle including some form of physical activity, healthy diet, and adequate sleep.

4.  Learn to be more assertive (less passive or less aggressive).

5. Learn to be more positive about yourself if your self-esteem or confidence is low.

6. Try not to overburden yourself with additional stress at any particular time.

7. Maintain a strong support system of friends and family to deal with major stressful life events.

8. Take time to get away from heavy demands and pressures to unwind.

9. Avoid negative habits such as using alcohol, drugs, cigarettes, or food to relieve stress.

10. Try to enhance your regular stress management skills with either a mindfulness or positive psychology approach, both of which are generally effective in improving resilience (see Chapter 8 for an overview of these methods).

It would be unrealistic for anyone to follow all of these recommenda- tions. The important point here is to make as many of these changes as you can reasonably do at this time. Taking these preventive steps in the near future and regularly using the iCope strategies should pro- vide a well-balanced approach to improving your coping skills **and** maintaining your health and well-being.

## COULD WHAT YOU EAT HELP YOU COPE?

It has often been recommended that we decrease our use of caffeine and make other dietary changes to help keep our stress in check. For years we have also talked about how eating helps "soothe the emotions." As discussed in Chapter 1, eating can clearly be unhealthy when used excessively as a coping method. Although the soothing effects of eating might be simply due to all the biological changes such as increased blood flow to the digestive tract that take place after we eat, some interesting new research, which has implications for coping with stress, has shown a possible link between the gut and the brain.

Various neuro-scientists have researched the link between certain probiotic bacteria (like those found in yogurt and available in pill form at health food stores) and stress in animals. Rats fed a high probiotic diet were compared to a normal control group of rats on a regular diet. The two groups were given a stress test in water where they had to swim in a bowl where they could not escape. Although rats are natural swimmers, they seem to hate being in water! The rats in the control group showed the intense fight-or-flight reaction and swam vigorously for about four minutes and then gave up and simply floated on the water. This "giving up" response is referred to as *behavioral defeat* or *learned helplessness*. The probiotic fed rats showed the same initial reaction, but seemed to calm down after a couple of minutes and continued to swim actively until the researchers took them out of the water bowl. Later research showed that there was a neural connection between the brain and gut via the vagus nerve. How this process works is still unknown, but it appears that rats on probiotic diets have an increase in the brain's level of GABA, an inhibitory neurotransmitter that calms the nervous system.

We do not know whether this research will prove to be consistent with humans. If it does, we might someday see refined recommendations of which foods, probiotics, etc. will be recommended as a true dietary way to help us manage stress.

## SUMMARY OF iCope PROCEDURES

You can learn to manage your stress level within minutes by practicing the following five steps that have been described in the book.

1. **TUNE IN TO YOUR STRESS LEVEL**. Improve your self-awareness. Rate your stress from **1** (very relaxed) to **10** (very stressed). If you have a biofeedback card, it will help you gauge your stress level. Whenever you feel tense, proceed with the rest of the steps.

2. **RELAX**! Take a deep breath that extends your stomach, hold it for 4-5 seconds, breathe out slowly through your mouth while saying "calm" or "cope" to yourself. Repeat this a second time.

3. **TALK RATIONALLY TO YOURSELF**. "What's making me so stressed? It's probably not as bad as I think. I've handled situations like this before. I can calm myself and feel better later." Challenge any of your *irrational* beliefs. Avoid negative mental habits such as overgeneralizing, catastrophizing, expecting too much, or focusing on the negative. Keep things in perspective.

4. **PROBLEM SOLVE**. Often there are ways to reduce your distress. Think about your options. Avoid saying *"nothing can be done."* Be an "active coper" and take control of whatever you can. What can you do soon to feel better without getting yourself into trouble? Pick an option and try it. If it doesn't help, try another until you feel better. Stay flexible and be creative.

5. **RECHECK YOUR STRESS LEVEL**. If you reduced your stress, even slightly, take credit for a job well done. Check to see if you reached your *effective stress zone*. If your stress remains high, remind yourself it takes practice. When the time is right, go back to Step 2 and repeat the procedure. With practice you will get better.

# STRESS SCALE

**1 2 3 4 5 6 7 8 9 10**
Very Relaxed   Alert   Very Stressed

# CHAPTER **8**

## *Enhancing Success: Mindfulness and Positive Psychology*

Much of this book has been devoted to teaching various skills to help manage the inevitable stress that occurs in our daily lives. As was discussed in the introduction to the book, stress is a natural part of our lives and in the correct balance this can be positive. Stress can be a serious problem when there is too much of it over an extended period of time, and the person does not manage it successfully. Although many of the skills taught in this book such as relaxing or talking rationally to yourself when you are stressed might seem like "reactive" ways to deal with troublesome stress, it is also helpful to keep a much broader perspective of how we cope with stress.

Taking a look at your lifestyle is sometimes needed in order to see other proactive steps that could improve your coping skills or, more importantly, improve your resilience to stress. From this more holistic approach, we as individuals can do a variety of things that will prepare us to withstand potential difficulties in our lives. Although there are many factors in our lifestyle such as social opportunities, nutrition, physical exercise, and even financial security that are important, our focus here is on some of the major psychological advances that would be important to consider. Two approaches will be highlighted here. One of these is "**mindfulness training**" which focuses more on self-awareness and deeper relaxation experiences; the other is a broader movement called "**positive psychology**." Both of these approaches are well established and have considerable research to support their overall effectiveness in improving our resilience, happiness, health, and the ability to cope.

## MINDFULNESS TRAINING

Although mindfulness training has been established for many years, it has been receiving more research, attention, and acceptance throughout the country in the past decade. In addition to being used in many medical centers, mindfulness is being taught in companies and even school systems. Although we can provide a description of what mindfulness is, if you have the opportunity, it is ideal to experience it in a workshop or class if it is available in your community or school. Sometimes an intellectual discussion of something like mindfulness does not convey the "experience" which is much more important. A personal example will help illustrate this. When I was learning to fly a single engine plane, my flight instructor in one lesson said he wanted me to "see" what could happen under certain conditions in flight. This all sounded interesting until we got to about 8,000 feet where he purposely put the plane into a downward spiral toward the ground! After his first successful demonstration, he then let me handle the next spin. Then we practiced this a few more times. The method to his madness was very sound and helpful in my training since I had all of the visual cues, physical sensations, and emotional reactions to this experience which could **not** be taught by reading a book or an instruction manual. Fortunately for me, this training was necessary and actually saved my life one day when I was flying solo and my plane went into a spin that I successfully handled. The reason for this story is that mindfulness is something you have to experience (rather than just read about) in order to get a full appreciation of its usefulness.

Jon Kabat-Zinn (2012), the founder of Mindfulness-Based Stress Reduction at the University of Massachusetts Medical Center over 35 years ago, describes this as a way of *purposely and non-judgmentally paying attention in a particular way to what you are experiencing in the present moment*. One way to understand this is to try to purposely focus your attention (mind) on what you are experiencing. For example, if you closed your eyes and began to focus on your breathing, you would pay attention to the sensations, movement, and physiological reactions that you experience. You do not want to judge the experience such as "Oh wow, my breathing is too fast or slow." You would just try to attend to your experience. Close your eyes and do that for the next 20-30 seconds. Check out what it feels like. You might notice warmth, heaviness, or other sensations in parts of your body, and you would be "mindful" of that experience. You might also notice that you have certain emotional reactions that might be comforting like calmness, but you might also feel uncomfortable in other ways. This is where the "non-judgemental" aspect of mindfulness becomes important. You want to become aware of your sensations and feelings, but you do not want to attribute any judgement to that experience. For example, you would not want to be thinking something negative like, "There must be something wrong since I cannot get calm or relaxed doing this." Prior to the exercise you would be breathing without any conscious awareness of it. During the exercise you become "mindful" of the breathing experience. Again, the purpose of mindfulness is to **focus your attention on the experience in the present moment without judging it in any way**. A potential and beneficial byproduct of mindfulness is that when you focus attention on a current experience, you cannot be worrying or thinking about past or future problems.

Some of the basic exercises in mindfulness training are aimed at teaching a form of meditation to help you learn how to focus attention. In this process, people will achieve deep levels of relaxation. This part of mindfulness training clearly would help you with two of our iCope skills - *self awareness* and *physical relaxation*. However, mindfulness training is much more than just relaxation training. You could practice mindful eating, walking, taking a shower, sitting at your desk, etc.

---

### A FIVE-MINUTE MINDFUL EXERCISE

*The following exercise is one of the most basic ones used as an introduction to mindfulness. This is quite different than the relaxation exercise in Chapter 4 where you were asked to focus on something like a word or a visual scene. In mindful breathing you are simply focusing your attention on the act of breathing and noticing what that experience feels like. It is described here, but if you have access to the internet, listen to a sample of the instructions that will enhance the experience. (**http://www.icope. co**)*

*Get into a comfortable position, sitting up straight in your chair, or lie down if you prefer. I find that it is helpful if you close your eyes during this practice but if you do not feel comfortable doing that, keep your eyes open. Begin to focus on your breathing, paying attention to each breath as you inhale and exhale. You can breathe in and out through your nose if that is more comfortable, or inhale through your nose and exhale through your mouth. As you settle into your mindful breathing, simply pay attention to what you experience. Notice any sensations. It also helps to pay attention to how your breathing is being done. Check to see if you are using your belly as you breathe in and out. Using your belly (actually your diaphragm) does seem*

---

*to help with relaxation. If you put your hands on your belly, you most likely will feel your belly expand as you breathe in and it will compress when you exhale. Sometimes emphasizing this type of breathing feels even more relaxing.*

*Focus on your breathing for about 4-5 minutes. A normal part of this exercise is that you will find that your mind will wander. You might start thinking about other things, typically from the past or things you need to do in the future. Noticing aches, pains, and physical sensations, or paying attention to sounds around you is also likely to happen. This is normal and to be expected. You simply want to catch yourself when your mind drifts, and try to focus gently back on your breathing. Remember, this is a non-judgmental experience so there is not a good or bad experience. Over the five minutes you will learn what the experience feels like. Try to do this at various times throughout the week to see if it leads to a sense of peacefulness or well-being. This will give you a little sample of what mindful breathing is like. If you take a mindfulness class, your teacher/leader will work with you to increase the amount of time that you can devote to this breathing exercise.*

Full mindfulness programs have been used to enhance health, relationships, productivity at work, as well as performance skills by athletes, musicians, artists, and stage performers. It is not within the scope of this chapter to give a comprehensive overview of mindfulness training and all of its potential benefits. Our hope is that if you believe that this type of training could help you in various ways, you will seek out some additional resources to try this approach. Since more hospitals, universities, and schools are offering these programs, you might find an introductory workshop or program in your community. There are also several books on the topic and some of these are listed in the reference section. There are also many YouTube clips of talks by Jon Kabat-Zinn and others on mindfulness.

## POSITIVE PSYCHOLOGY

*P*ositive psychology is a second approach that takes a broader per-spective that can also help us in our efforts to manage stress in our lives and improve our resilience. Positive psychology is **not** focused on stress disorders, illness or mental health problems. It is aimed at understanding many other proactive approaches including how we can improve happiness, optimism, meaning, contentment, a sense of control, and well-being in our lives.

The pre-eminent researcher and writer about this broad move-ment within psychology is Martin Seligman at the University of Pennsylvania. After decades of research and several books focused on depression, learned optimism, and happiness, he has synthesized his work in a recent book (*Flourish: A Visionary New Understanding of Happiness and Well-Being*, 2011). He has been a leading force in devel-oping the field of positive psychology to a point where it is now one of the most popular classes at many universities. As you will see, posi-tive psychology is NOT walking around forcing a smile on your face all the time, or sitting around waiting for positive things to happen to you just because you want them to happen. This is also more than telling yourself positive affirmations to make yourself feel "better." These are misconceptions that can over simplify the true nature of positive psychology.

## THE MODEL FOR WELL-BEING

*Within this larger context of positive psychology, Seligman's model describes the importance of "**well-being**" and how we can develop this. Although he is not saying this is the way to cope with day-to-day stress, his model of well-being in our opinion is clearly something that can help increase your resilience, transition beyond traumatic events, and reinforce any stress management efforts that you are making. In this model, Seligman believes that well-being is composed of five measurable elements that can be remembered with the mnemonic PERMA. The five elements are: **P**ositive emotions, **E**ngagement, **R**elationships that are positive, **M**eaning, and **A**ccomplishment.*

***Positive emotions** are what we typically think of as the good feelings or sensations such as "happiness" "pleasure" or "life satisfaction." **Engagement** refers to the state of being able to be fully absorbed in something that is very important to you. Maintaining **positive relationships** is a powerful element in developing our well-being. As stated by Seligman, "Other people are the best antidote to the downs of life and the single most reliable up." **Meaning** refers to the sense that you belong to, serve, and have an impact on something bigger than yourself. **Accomplishment** is the element of well-being that centers on pursuing success, attaining achievement in some important area of life, or developing mastery in some area. Golf anyone?*

According to this approach, well-being, and not happiness alone, is the goal in positive psychology. As stated by Seligman, "... well-being is a combination of feeling good (*positive emotions and engagement*) as well as having meaning, good relationships, and accomplishment. The way we choose our course in life is to maximize all five of these elements." If you look closely at this approach, you will see that it would enhance your resilience to stress. Positive emotions and relationships are extremely important in well-being, but these are just as essential in how we can buffer ourselves from the impact of a variety of stressors. Similarly, having meaning and a sense of accomplishment or achievement will have a tremendous impact on self-esteem and confidence, both of which are so critical in stress management. Thus, effective stress management enhances our well-being, and well-being in turn helps improve the resilience needed to protect us from the negative effects of stress. These two approaches go hand in hand.

Like everything else discussed in this book, it is important to keep "happiness" and "well-being" in perspective. These are not "cure alls" for every problem, issue, or negative event that we will encounter. We cannot expect to always be happy since there will be demanding stressful challenges, important losses, or major life events to confront in a lifetime. If relationships are so important to us, then we undoubtedly will have to cope with those instances when we lose a relationship. If achievement helps our well-being, there may be setbacks where everything does not go as planned in our education, career, or personal development. If you are able to develop important healthy relationships and engage in meaningful pursuits toward important goals throughout your life, this will certainly lead to being content (i.e., happy) with life. At the same time, your coping skills give you the ability to handle day-to-day stress and the added resilience needed for major stressors. However, we cannot maintain any unrealistic expectations that we will always be stress free and happy. Some research suggests that having some, but not too many, of these stressful challenges actually does improve our ability to handle future stress. Maybe there is some truth to the old adage: "What doesn't kill you makes you stronger."

What are some steps to take to enhance happiness or well-being? The answer to this can easily involve taking a course in positive psychology or reading some of the books on the topic. Here we can only give a sample of a few exercises that research shows has a positive effect on well-being or happiness.

## Gratitude

I was attending a Psychology convention a number of years ago and by chance saw the professor, Dr. Warren Steinman, who taught my first undergraduate class in psychology at Denison University. He had a profound influence in my introduction to psychology and my eventual decision to pursue graduate work in the field. We had not seen each other for at least 20 years prior to this chance meeting, so he clearly had no idea who I was. I took the opportunity when I saw him to approach him, introduce myself as a former student, and explain how big a role he played in my life. I thanked him for being such a great teacher and positive influence in my career path. At the time, I did not know how important expressing gratitude would become in the field of positive psychology. I just knew it was what I wanted to share with my former professor, and I knew it felt good to give him my feedback. It also looked like it felt good for him to hear from me. Look back at your life so far. Is there anyone to whom you can express your sense of gratitude? Have you expressed it in any way? If so, try to remember how it felt when you did this.

The research over the past few years on the importance of gratitude has consistently shown positive effects. One of the most powerful exercises is to write a "gratitude letter" to someone who has had a positive impact on you. In the ideal situation, you ask the person if you can meet with them and share your letter. This exercise typically demonstrates how important the *practice of showing gratitude* is in improving your overall emotional state. It is recommended that you look for opportunities to share gratitude in less formal ways on a regular basis with friends, co-workers and family. Grateful people typically see life as being more satisfactory and focus on what they have rather than what is missing in their lives.

## Count Your Blessings

Since we often tend to overlook many of the positive things we have going for us, it is helpful to spend some time looking at what we are thankful for in our personal lives. You can do this in a number of ways. You can begin to do your own inventory of positive things in your life whether these are relationships of all sorts, personal characteristics, skills and abilities, accomplishments, the environment you live in, even material possessions, etc. Keep a running log of these blessings in a notebook since you are likely to forget many items that could be listed at any given moment. By keeping an ongoing list, you will see the list grow in the days and weeks ahead. Periodically review your list as a reminder of the positive people, places, and things in your life.

Alternatively, Seligman recommends that you take ten minutes before you go to sleep at night to write down three positive things you are thankful for during the day. Try this for a week or more to see if you become more aware of your blessings.

## Further Steps

In addition to these two exercises there are many other things you can try in order to begin to benefit from the philosophy espoused in positive psychology. Here is a brief list:

1. Do random acts of kindness when you see the opportunities.

2. Volunteer to work with a local organization to help the under-privileged.

3.  Become a mentor as a big brother or big sister in your community.

4.  Participate in a fund raising campaign for a meaningful charity or group.

5.  In addition to continuing all the activities that regularly bring you emotional happiness, try to develop a menu of additional experiences that bring you joy. For example, read the daily comics in your newspaper or online, find entertaining TV shows or movies to enjoy with friends, or collect a set of humorous YouTube clips on your computer that you can use whenever you want to feel better.

6.  Develop a new skill or rekindle an old interest that you think you could become passionate about, especially those that involve other people. Learn a new enjoyable game (chess, backgammon, cards, etc.), a skill (cooking, photography, etc.) or hobby (e.g., SCUBA diving, fishing, golf, tennis).

7.  Actively look for something you can do that a family member or close friend would not expect, but would make them happy or grateful toward you.

Although you do not have to do all of these things to be happy and resilient to stress, some combination of these efforts is likely to have a significant positive impact on your mood and life satisfaction.

# Supplement A:

## *Assertiveness and Anger Management*

As you will recall from Chapter 1, stressors trigger the *fight-or-flight* response. Since many stressful events do involve other people, each one of us is likely to have this fight-or-flight reaction in many different social situations throughout our lives. In order to deal with people in these stressful situations, we tend to develop a preferred pattern of handling ourselves when we encounter conflicts. These behavior patterns can be so strong that they appear to dominate the personality of some individuals.

Some people respond with aggression or some other type of hostile attitude when they are frustrated or stressed by others. Anger and hostility dominate their emotions. These individuals are likely to stand up for their rights, but frequently at the expense of others. They can be verbally or even physically abusive. This "fight" pattern sometimes does get aggressive individuals what they want. However, this also tends to chase people away or leads to counter-aggression from others. The end result is that the aggressive person has difficulty maintaining **satisfying** long-term relationships.

Another group of individuals tend to respond primarily with the "flight" reaction. Here the person is likely to shy away from conflict with others and to avoid confrontations at all costs. Fear and anxiety seem to be their dominant emotions. In extreme cases, the person might be too passive or withdrawn. These individuals seldom express their opinions, ideas, beliefs, or feelings. Because of this pattern, they are often taken advantage of by others. They often will give in to peer pressure to be accepted. It is not uncommon for a very passive individual to have occasional outbursts of aggression whenever the stress level builds to intolerable levels. After these aggressive outbursts, the person goes back to the basic passive pattern.

## ASSERTIVE BEHAVIOR

Although these two basic patterns (*aggressive* and *passive*) seem to be natural expressions of the fight-or-flight response, there is a more adaptive alternative in today's society. This pattern, often called **assertiveness** or **assertive behavior**, involves a number of behaviors that help the individual cope with stress and deal more effectively with others. Assertiveness includes being able to:

1. express thoughts, opinions, and feelings in an honest and direct way;
2. stand up for your rights;
3. make a request;
4. give **positive or negative** feedback to others including family and friends;
5. accept positive or negative feedback from others;
6. express an honest opinion that is different from others;
7. not allow others to take advantage of you; and
8. say "no" when you want to.

Engaging in assertive behavior will not always get you what you want, although it will maximize your chances in most situations. However, even when assertiveness does not get direct results, there are some indirect positive outcomes. First, you become more active and less helpless in dealing with other people in stressful situations. This is a more healthy approach from both a physical and a psychological standpoint. Second, you are likely to improve your confidence and gain the respect of others since assertiveness appears to be more socially desirable than aggression or passivity. This in turn usually leads to more positive self-esteem.

Finally, being assertive is likely to improve your communication skills that can prevent many future stressful conflicts. For those individuals who see themselves as too passive or too aggressive, it is suggested that you read one of the recommended books on assertiveness or attend a workshop or class on the subject in your school or local community.

Learning to be more assertive is a major social skill that will supplement your stress management efforts. In your problem solving exercises you are also likely to find that many alternatives can be some form of assertive behavior. This is especially important with your most significant relationships such as those with family members and close friends.

## ANGER MANAGEMENT

The topic of *anger management* has gotten much attention in various books, TV shows, and movies. However, the issues, skills, and treatment approaches are virtually identical to stress management. As you know by now, anger and aggressive behavior are components of the stress reaction, specifically the *fight-or-flight* reaction. Clearly, anger management will require basic stress management skills plus additional attention to the situations that lead to aggression. There is also concern about the serious consequences that aggression creates in various interpersonal relationships. The reason the discussion is included here with assertiveness is because assertive behavior is another primary skill that an aggressive person needs to learn. Using our model of stress and assertiveness, what, if anything, is different with anger management?

In our basic model, the chronically angry or hostile person appears to be operating under a generally high level of stress. They may be close to their threshold on our stress scale such that small events can trigger a big reaction. When we hear expressions like "He really has a short fuse" or "She is a hot reactor," we can easily see how being close to threshold can give others this impression. The person is likely to have outbursts of aggression, either verbally or physically. These are extremely negative coping responses that might only work in the short run to defuse a heightened emotional state. In the long run the consequences can be devastating in terms of the problems created in interpersonal relationships. An angry person is likely to seem threatening and unpredictable to others, which obviously is not helpful in any relationship.

Outbursts of aggressive behavior will also lead to other problems. Others will often start to avoid the angry person. Occasionally, the aggressive behavior will lead to counter-aggression which can escalate to dangerous levels. Intimate relationships can be destroyed easily. An educational or career path can also be ruined or stunted by inappropriate expressions of anger. Serious problems where the anger leads to legal problems, physical aggression, road rage, or disciplinary action at school require professional help as soon as possible. For those whose anger is not a danger to others, there are some recommendations that might help. The following guidelines are for those readers who need to control their aggressive behavior.

First, if you need help with anger management, you have to be <u>exceptionally</u> skilled in your ability to gauge your stress level (*self-awareness*). As mentioned above, it is likely that your baseline stress level is close to your threshold for aggressive behavior. Since you are vulnerable to small events that can trigger an over-reaction, you will benefit from learning to bring that baseline level down on a regular basis. If you are operating at a 7-8 stress level through much of the day, set a realistic goal of reducing that by 1 or 2 points. Some individuals can do this simply with *more frequent* practice of the breathing and relaxation methods. Take *several* one-minute breaks throughout the day to check your stress level and take a few deep breaths to bring your stress level down. This is important even when you are not consciously aware of any stress that is present. Other individuals may need the more active physical outlets by increasing aerobic activity or physical exertion throughout the week.

Second, work more diligently on identifying your mental habits and irrational beliefs that set you up for anger. We have all heard the expression that other people really know how to push your **buttons**. If this rings true for you, it is highly likely that you do have certain *irrational beliefs* and/or *mental habits* that exacerbate your stress response. Often it is some comment or question that taps into a **perceived flaw** in you, or a **perceived rejection** from someone else. In other situations, others do not behave as you expect and this elicits anger due to a **perceived failure** on their part.

As we learned in the chapter on rational self-talk, when we tell ourselves something *irrational*, the stress will be magnified. This is the mechanism that is typically operating when buttons are being easily pushed. For example, if someone makes a relatively harmless comment or asks a simple question, you might misinterpret the message. If someone such as your teacher or a parent comments on some task or responsibility that you did **not** complete, how would you react? Would you angrily tell yourself – and maybe even them – anything negative that would lead you to over react? Pay particular attention to comments or negative self-talk such as: "Do you think I'm stupid?"; "Who are you to tell me what to do?"; "You can't control me."; or "Do you think you're so perfect?" These types of thoughts suggest that beliefs about needing *to be thoroughly competent and perfect,* beliefs about *another person's right to ask you a question or give you negative feedback,* or beliefs about *being approved by others* are consciously or unconsciously making your anger worse.

Because there is a high probability that you harbor some of these and possibly other irrational beliefs (*buttons*) that inflame your emotions, you need to exert extra effort to challenge these self-statements. Look for the specific situations that trigger anger and keep copies of your Stress Analysis Chart available. *Detailed written notes* of your negative self-statements over a more *extended time period* will give you more opportunities to practice your rational self-talk in anger-provoking situations. This is an extremely important skill since you need to react quickly to those surprise bursts of anger that catch you off guard.

The third set of anger management skills includes various **behavioral strategies** to prevent or short circuit an angry outburst. The old adage recommending that we count to 10 when we are upset is representative of this major behavioral strategy: you need time away from the anger-provoking situation to use some other appropriate coping skills to get things under better control. The reality is that we often need to count much higher than 10! One of the basic skills here is the use of a self-initiated **"time out"** procedure. This is particularly important for your most important relationships where you can discuss beforehand what you are going to do with the *time out* procedure. If you discuss your strategy prior to implementing it, most people will find this to be a very positive step.

When you actually take a *time out,* it is best to let the other person know in the calmest way possible that: 1) you cannot continue with the discussion or the situation, and 2) that you will excuse yourself for a period of time. There is flexibility in how long you stay "away" and where you go at these times. To maximize the benefits for your relationships, it is best not to take these time outs for extended periods. No, you cannot go on a week vacation for a time out! You want others to know that you will return within a reasonable period of time to discuss whatever led to the anger-provoking situation. A general guideline would be to limit the time out to no more than an hour or two unless the situation is so volatile that you need extended time before you can handle the discussions. Also, it is generally recommended that you do not leave in your car (even if you have a driver's license). It is sometimes helpful to do something physical during your time out: go for a walk or bike ride, do some chore around the house, or if you are at school get permission to talk to a school counselor or teacher who you trust.  Since this is not like a child's time out, you can also listen to some music, play a video game, go online, or watch TV. This time out procedure can be a very healthy behavioral method to cope with anger and aggression.

To work best, remember to discuss your new strategy in advance of your initial effort to use it in any close relationships. Keep in mind that others may see signals of your increased frustration and anger before you do. Therefore, it is also very important to *give the other person the right to call "time out" if he or she believes it is necessary, and for you to honor these requests.*

A fourth strategy is sometimes difficult to implement, but it can be very powerful in defusing anger.  There is a well-established psychological principle that you cannot feel two competing emotions at the same time. For example, you cannot experience fear and relaxation simultaneously. Similarly, humor and anger seem to be incompatible emotions. To use this in anger management you need a particular *thought* or *image* that is so humorous that it puts a smile on your face or makes you laugh. In order to generate some humorous images, it is sometimes helpful to get and review your own personal collection of funny YouTube clips on your computer. If you can conjure up a funny thought or an image when you are *beginning to feel angry*, the humor will help dissipate your anger. To be successful, try to use this method first when you feel mild irritations or frustrations to get practice for those times when you need to defuse more intense anger.

Finally, some preventive steps can help prepare you for high-risk situations. Many of us can predict some typical times or situations that frequently lead to frustration and anger. If you are aware of any of these high risk times, it is recommended that you practice some of the coping procedures **prior** to encountering the situation. For example, if one of your teachers provokes anger, do your breathing exercises and rational self-talk *before* you go to class. This will help get your baseline level a little lower as you enter the stressful situation. Teens and parents often report that the most stressful time for encountering each other is shortly after they see each other at the end of the school/work day. In these situations you can avoid some of the difficulties by agreeing that after you greet each other, you will **NOT** discuss anything important until the last person entering the home has had about 20-30 minutes to defuse from daily events.

In summary, there are eight key recommendations for the person needing anger management:

1. If your behavior is a serious problem for those at school or home, seek professional help in conjunction with the following steps.
2. Practice your basic coping strategies on a more frequent basis. Become highly alert and aware of your stress level, practice the relaxation methods throughout the day, and use the Stress Analysis Charts regularly to determine your irrational beliefs or **buttons**.
3. Implement a self-imposed time out procedure.
4. Have a list of behavioral options you can use when an aggressive reaction is likely. Although this often involves removing yourself from the situation until you are calmer, there may be other options (e.g., assertive behavior) that will help.
5. If you can, begin to use humor to help dissipate anger.
6. Practice the assertive skills discussed earlier in this section.
7. Read one of the books on assertive training and anger listed in the recommended reading list.
8. Implement some preventive steps that will help you prepare for high-risk situations.

Using these eight steps will give you a well-balanced approach to anger management. Again, if the self-help strategies do not work effectively, it is likely that some consultation with a professional who specializes in stress and anger management will be helpful.

# Supplement **B**:

## *Time Management and Organizational Skills*

For any busy person, a major source of stress is having too much work to do in a limited amount of time. Taking steps to manage your time more effectively can help reduce this pressure. Here are some basic suggestions.

1. **Become aware of how you spend your time**. Keeping a daily log of time usage for a week sometimes produces surprising results. Use this step to learn where you *waste time*. When done excessively, some of the most common *time wasters* are:

   telephone calls
   running errands
   texting constantly
   fixing mistakes of others
   watching TV
   daydreaming
   napping
   internet surfing

playing video games
checking Facebook, e-mail, or Twitter too frequently

It is clear that many of these are enjoyable activities, but they are considered *time wasters* when they interfere with your primary goals, major obligations, or responsibilities.

2. **Set some priorities on how you want to maximize use of your time**. This often will be based on your longer-term goals. This does not mean that you cannot enjoy any of the activities listed above. What it does mean is that you have to find the right **balance** in how these can fit into your overall priorities.

3. **Take an active step to decrease time wasters**. Spend more of your time on high priority activities that will lead toward your ultimate goals. The following methods can help you do this more successfully.

   **a. Get organized**. Clear your desk or work area. Eliminate any distracting material that is not relevant to your immediate task. Get into the habit of having things in their place and have your books, class notes, and study materials in order.

   **b. Begin making daily or weekly *to do lists***. This is best done in the evening. Spending as little as 5-10 minutes a day on this step will be a good investment of your time and will help you stay organized. Plan out your week so you can maintain awareness of exam/quiz dates, papers due, work schedules, etc. so you can make effective *to-do lists*.

   **c. Rate each item** on a 3-point rating system. Since there are major differences in the importance of the many things that can end up on your "to do" list, rate options in the following way: #1 items are most critical; #2 items are somewhat important; and #3 items are the least important. Since we have a tendency to

100

avoid spending time on difficult tasks, you might find that you are avoiding high priority tasks and spending too much of your time on less important tasks. Therefore, it is *generally recommended* that you maximize the amount of time you spend on the #1 items. When you complete a task, check it off and move on to the next #1 task. When you complete all your #1 items, then move to #2 tasks. Obviously, you need considerable flexibility to determine what is most critical since schedules and assignments can frequently change. Others, such as your parents or teachers, may require a task to be completed promptly, which will shift other tasks to the top of your to do list.

**d. Become highly efficient when you are working on a task.** If you are distracted in certain areas of your house, find a less distracting place to study or work on important assignments. Temporarily avoid phone calls, texting, e-mails, etc. when you are trying to focus on high priority projects. If your room has too many distractions, try to find a "neutral" place in your house (e.g., your dining room), or nearby (e.g., a library), when you need to focus on lengthy or complicated tasks.

**e. Learn to be assertive.** This is especially important if you have trouble saying *"no."* If refusing a request will help you avoid doing something that will waste time or take away from your high priority activities, you might want to be appropriately assertive and say *no*. You will find that being direct and open about your priorities with others is necessary to get the best use of your time.

4. **Periodically re-evaluate how you are spending time.** Are you accomplishing your priorities? Are there any major time wasters that continue to take away from your efforts? Are you staying organized? When you see patterns shifting back to inefficient time use, try to remedy the situation as quickly as you can.

These steps can help you make some adjustments in how you use your time. Obviously you have to be motivated to want to spend time on activities like school work that might not be enjoyable. Keep your long-term goals in perspective since that might help reinforce your efforts. Also, remember that this is not an all-or-none approach. You will want to maintain a good balance of responsible behavior and your leisure/recreational time.

# Supplement C:

## *Building Self-Esteem and Confidence*

Although the term "self-esteem" is a very general term, most of us have a pretty good idea of the concept and how it relates to us personally. If someone asks "How would you rate your self-esteem?" think about your answer. Does it reflect that you generally think positively about yourself, or do you hesitate and answer with a lot of cautionary statements about your flaws or deficits? What does it mean if we think we have low self-esteem? Clearly it would be better in many ways if we have generally *positive* or *high* self-esteem. To see how self-esteem could have an impact on you or your friends, briefly list how **low self-esteem** would affect anyone in the following areas:

Your thoughts/opinions about yourself:

Your emotions:

Your behavior:

Your social life:

As you would expect, all of these areas are affected by **low self-esteem**. In extreme situations, very *negative thoughts* and opinions such as: "I'm a loser," "I'm not good enough, successful enough, or attractive enough" could be present. Depression, anxiety, fear, and anger would be common *emotional reactions. Behavioral patterns* can range from withdrawal and isolation due to fear of rejection, to acting out rebelliously in some way through your clothing, appearance, eating behavior, or engaging in inappropriate sexual behavior to get acceptance or attention. Finally, your *social life* will be affected. You might be less assertive and less willing to try to expand your circle of friends. If this continues for years, the typical social skills that would be good to develop in your teen and young adult years can be severely delayed. Obviously, with so many problems that can be linked to low self-esteem, it is important to correct it because it causes so much unnecessary stress in a person's life even in later years.

The primary reason we have included this section is not just because low self-esteem causes stress, but also because most of the principles and methods of stress management can be used to correct and improve self-esteem as well. A final reason for discussing self-esteem is that this will improve self-confidence, which has been shown to improve *resilience* to stress. Although a full discussion of the development of self-esteem is beyond the scope of this section, it is safe to accept the fact that our self-esteem is shaped by our life experiences, feedback from others, and the beliefs and perceptions we eventually learn to hold about ourselves. For further discussion of this and related topics, please check the recommended readings.

## COGNITIVE FACTORS IN SELF-ESTEEM

In Chapter 5 on **Talking Rationally to Yourself**, we discussed mental habits such as *catastrophizing, overgeneralizing, focusing on the negative*, and maintaining *excessive expectations* that increase stress. In addition to these, additional mental habits are particularly important to self-esteem. The three additional patterns discussed by Schiraldi (2000) that can erode self-esteem are: *labeling, rejecting positive feedback*, and *making unfavorable comparisons*. If you give yourself *negative label*s such as "loser," "jerk," "unattractive," or "failure," this will definitely affect your self-esteem. If you hold on to those labels, new life experiences like doing poorly in a class or having a relationship end will then reinforce the label or self-image. Holding onto a negative label forces you into an all-or none view of yourself. Use the cognitive coping skills in Chapter 5 to counter a negative label as an *"irrational belief."* If you hold onto any negative labels, you need to begin challenging the basis of those specific beliefs as soon as possible.

The second mental habit discussed by Schiraldi is *rejecting positive feedback,* which can be a mental habit as well as a behavioral habit. Individuals with low self-esteem psychologically filter out positive comments or feedback since it does not fit with their perception of themselves. Behaviorally these individuals react to positive feedback or compliments by discounting them, saying things like "Oh, I was just lucky," or "It wasn't that big a deal." If this is the case for you, you want to start accepting positive messages. It's much better when complimented to say something like "Thank you, I appreciate that," or "It was nice of you to say that," which are both more assertive responses. Try to practice both mentally and behaviorally accepting positive messages from others.

The third mental habit that is damaging to self-esteem is *making unfavorable comparisons* between yourself and others. From a rational perspective, it is important to recognize that all of us can find others who are "better" with respect to certain qualities. However, this is not the measure of **your** self-esteem. It would be irrational to think that you could compare favorably to everyone else on all or even most of your personal qualities. Each of us has to do our own inventory of our self and begin to value those areas in which we are satisfied, proud, and genuinely positive. None of us can be perfect, but each of us must learn to recognize our qualities that are positive.

In addition to the mental habits discussed above, there are two troublesome irrational *beliefs* (also discussed in Chapter 5) that are particularly damaging to self-esteem.

1.  *I need to be thoroughly competent or perfect in everything I do.*
2.  *I need to be accepted by everyone who is important to me.*

Both of these beliefs are quite common in our culture. However, it will be very helpful to your self-esteem to begin challenging these thoughts if you hold on to either belief. The Stress Analysis Chart in Chapter 5 is a useful tool to challenge your irrational beliefs.

## BEHAVIORAL FACTORS IN SELF-ESTEEM

The cognitive factors discussed above focus on irrational beliefs and mental habits that damage self-esteem. Behavioral factors focus on things you are <u>doing</u> or <u>not doing</u> that make you upset about yourself. Although none of us is perfect, it does not mean that we cannot improve in certain behavioral ways if this is important to our self-esteem. For example, if you have very few hobbies or extracurricular activities, and this limits your confidence or social contacts, you could identify some behavioral changes that could improve this. You could learn a new skill (e.g., playing chess or pool) that then opens other social opportunities. If you are not very athletic and if playing a sport would improve your self-esteem, participating in a sport by taking lessons for an individual sport (e.g., tennis, golf, karate) or taking a chance on a team sport in school could be a positive step to take. However, you do not even have to participate in a sport to deal with your lack of athletic skills. You could accept the fact that you are not athletic using the cognitive methods, and focus on doing something that is more meaningful and positive to you. You could become a volunteer, learn to play a musical instrument, or join an after school club even though these have nothing to do with your athletic skills. The main point here is to *do positive things that enhance your self esteem.* See the Sidebar on Self-Control.

---

### *SELF-CONTROL*

*Although it is easy to say change your behavior if you do not like it, it is not that easy to follow through on many of our self-improvement efforts. How many people are actually successful in maintaining their New Years' resolutions? There are steps you can take to make you more successful in reaching any behavioral goal. First, try to be specific in setting your goals and make them realistic over time. Many New Years' resolutions are often not realistic, and this quickly sets them up for failure. Since many behavioral changes do take time to become well established, prepare yourself to look at reasonable time frames to reach your goals. You have to be patient in this process since it often takes months to make a behavioral change stable.*

*Second, share your plans with friends and family who will support your effort. Telling others about your goals can add positive motivation for you to follow through. At the same time, others are also more likely to reinforce your progress.*

---

*A third step that helps us persist in reaching a behavior goal is finding some measure of progress. Try to identify something you can monitor and track. If your goal is to improve grades, you might measure hours studying on a weekly basis, rather than wait six or more weeks to see if there is a grade change. Research shows that if you are trying to lose weight, quit smoking, reduce alcohol use, or make any other "specific" behavior change, simply keeping a record or graph of your progress will help in reaching your goal.*

*Even though reaching your goal is intrinsically reinforcing, the final step is to plan some additional reward for achieving your goal. Treat yourself to something pleasant or plan some type of celebration for your accomplishment. This can be on your own or with others if it was a particularly significant goal that you reached. This last step can be important for reaching smaller goals, so do what you can to add in these extra rewards.*

## SOCIAL FACTORS IN SELF-ESTEEM

In addition to the cognitive and behavioral factors that can enhance or hinder your self-esteem, social factors also play a key role in your self-esteem. Being accepted by others is likely to enhance both *social skills* and *self-esteem*. Although it is irrational to strive to be loved and accepted by everyone who is important to you, it is imperative to find and nurture some healthy social relationships throughout our lives. Learning the skills for positive well-balanced relationships is a key task to start developing in your teen years. These social skills are then refined throughout early adulthood. As was discussed in the section on positive psychology, positive social relationships are a key component to happiness and well-being.

In any discussion of social skills and relationships, it is important to keep in mind the notion that the quality of friendships, not quantity, is most important. It would be better to have one or two really close friends and a handful of good relationships than to be elected "prom queen." The key task is how to develop and maintain these quality relationships. We can offer some general suggestions here, but clearly you would want additional help or resources if you believe that you need to make big changes in your social life.

Probably the most basic principle is that any relationship requires each person to do certain things that nurture the relationship. All personal relationships are two-way streets that need positive reinforcement going both ways. If you are only the recipient of the positive things others provide to you, your relationship might last a while, but usually your friends will exit the relationship if there is little or nothing in it for them. Problems can develop if either party is too selfish or if there is little communication about what each person expects from the other.

If a relationship is important, try to learn what your friends expect from you, and communicate what you need from them. This kind of open discussion between friends is an important skill especially in more intimate relationships. This should help you find good balance in the relationships that are most important to you. Since there are no perfect relationships, each person has to be willing to compromise in meeting each other's needs and expectations.

Another basic principle is that conflict can arise even in most healthy relationships. Therefore, you have to be prepared to discuss problems if they are to be resolved. The earlier section on assertiveness may be helpful in addressing some of these situations. However, there will be times that regardless of how hard you try to compromise and resolve conflicts, the other party is <u>not willing or able</u> to change in any meaningful way. This obviously leads to a difficult choice. As Kenny Rogers said in one of his songs, *"You have to know when to hold 'em, and when to fold 'em."*

Clearly there will be times throughout life when you are forced to accept that a relationship is unsatisfactory and will not change. This could be one of the most difficult situations that you will face. At these times you will have to decide whether it is best for you to let go of an unhealthy relationship even though doing this will cause you anxiety, sadness, or even depression. In very difficult situations, it will help in the long term if you have the willingness and courage to end abusive, manipulative, or highly selfish relationships. Your overall self-esteem and confidence will benefit in the long run if you are able to successfully develop and handle relationships, whether they are healthy or conflicted. If you have trouble getting out of an unhealthy relationship, seek out help from trusted friends, family members, or even a counselor.

## SUMMARY

Your self-esteem is very important to your overall well-being in many ways. Use the principles in this section and in Chapter 5 to improve the way you evaluate yourself. *Avoid the mental traps and irrational beliefs* that limit your confidence and self-esteem. Take charge of the things about which you are dissatisfied and *change your behavior* whenever possible with reasonable goals and expectations of what you can change and what "imperfections" you need to accept about yourself. Since your social life will be an important factor in self-esteem, work to improve your own skills and develop the willingness to take the necessary risks to expand your social network to a level that is right for you. These cognitive, behavioral, and social skills developed earlier in life will be extremely helpful in many arenas throughout your lifetime. However, if you see that your self-esteem is seriously affecting your emotions or relationships, it would be wise to speak to a counselor or therapist for additional help.

# Supplement **D**:

## *Coping with Major Life Events*

**M**uch of this book is about how we can best cope with day-to-day stressors that are a regular part of life. However, there are times when something beyond our wildest expectations occurs that is very difficult to handle. These major life events are sometimes traumatic since they can be life threatening to you personally or to your friends and loved ones. Hopefully you never experience any of these events, but because they do occur, we want to briefly discuss how to cope with these most difficult situations.

There is a wide range of *traumatic events* that can occur. Some TV stations seem to relish showing us many of these events regardless of where they occur throughout the world. Traumatic events, which are sometimes called *critical incidents*, can include:

- Natural disasters – hurricanes, floods, tornadoes, or earthquakes;
- Terrorist events;
- Sexual assaults;

- Unexpected illness or death of a friend or family member;
- Life threatening events at your school, home, or work;
- Robberies;
- Mass casualty accidents;
- Being diagnosed with a serious illness.

There is much that we have learned in the last 30 years about how people react and cope with these major life events. TV news stations have often helped educate our country about the benefits of mental health counseling after natural disasters or deaths at school sites such as Columbine and Virginia Tech. Counseling was also widely promoted after national events like the terrorist attacks on 9/11 and other mass-casualty shootings like the ones in Tucson and Aurora. We also know that more isolated events such as accidents, rapes, murders, or other traumatic injuries can cause great difficulty for the survivors, family members, and witnesses of these events. Our reactions share many similarities regardless of the source of the trauma.

It should be noted here that what we learned about stress reactions to these traumatic life-threatening events also holds true for other **major life events**. All of the following events can cause a serious challenge to our coping abilities even though they are not necessarily life-threatening:

- Divorce of your parents;
- Loss of a long-term relationship;
- Moving to a new city and/or school;
- Leaving home for the first time to attend college;
- Joining the military.

This section covers information about post-traumatic reactions and what you can do to buffer yourself from the negative effects of these challenging situations. This chapter is educational in nature and is in no way meant to be a substitute for counseling or therapy if you experience a traumatic or major life event. If you believe that you are in need of counseling, you are encouraged to contact close family members, your primary care physicians, or spiritual advisors to get a referral to an appropriate therapist in your community.

## TYPICAL REACTIONS TO EXPECT

Similar to our discussion of *typical* reactions to everyday *stressors*, a number of common reactions will occur in more intense ways after a traumatic experience. The description below talks about traumatic events, but also refers to non-lethal critical incidents and major life events. Although more intense, these reactions often can be grouped into the same four categories that describe our typical stress reactions:

**PHYSICAL**
**EMOTIONAL**
**COGNITIVE**
**BEHAVIORAL**

The **physical reactions** to trauma include a queasy stomach, nausea, sweating, rapid breathing, muscle aches, chills, cold hands or feet, and rapid heart rates. If this state of heightened physiological arousal lasts too long, we may experience other complications such as headaches, diarrhea or constipation, hyperventilation, chest pain, muscular pain, or dizziness. Sleep disruption and loss of appetite are very common. If you have any physical ailments such as a history of asthma, heart attacks, or an autoimmune disorder, it is recommended that you contact your physician.

The **emotional reactions** to trauma include differing degrees of anxiety/fear, sadness/depression, anger, grief, guilt, and helplessness. Sometimes the emotions are hard to isolate and identify.

Individuals will say that they feel a general sense of being numb or overwhelmed. Although this heightened state of both physical and emotional arousal is a "normal" reaction to the traumatic event, much of the counseling effort by professionals is aimed at helping people cope with these emotions in a way that minimizes any risk of long term interference with the person's life. Simply venting strong emotions is not likely to make them go away for very long. Some of the sections below offer some guidance regarding how to improve your coping skills.

The **cognitive effects** of trauma are quite varied. Some of the most common reactions are temporary impairments of memory, concentration, attention, and problem solving. There may be a perception that "the events" are not real or we are having a bad dream. Time may seem distorted, especially during or shortly after the traumatic event. If we witnessed the event and felt very vulnerable at the time, we might have flashbacks or nightmares of the event. Intrusive thoughts about the event or issues related to it, worries, hyper-vigilance, and mistrust can also develop. As we begin to cope with the overall physical and emotional stress, we will often see our general cognitive abilities (e.g., attention, memory, concentration) improve as well, although this might take several days or weeks to occur depending on the event.

Whenever we have to adapt to some major change in our lives, including exposure to a traumatic event, we also have ***behavioral reactions*** that go along with the *physiological, emotional*, and *cognitive* changes. Some of these changes are aimed at helping us cope with the events, but they may not be effective in the long run. Some people will withdraw socially while others will want to spend time close to their loved ones. Some will avoid anything that increases their anxiety and may have trouble getting to school or work. Following through on basic responsibilities can become difficult. Increases in alcohol, drug use, and cigarette smoking can also occur.

114

As you can see there are numerous ways that we react to trauma. Although there are some similarities in how we react, it is important to remember that we are all individuals and differences are to be expected. Research clearly shows that those who are closest to the danger are likely to show the most extreme reactions. Those who are coping with other major losses or problems in their lives may have more difficulty coping with the trauma. Those who have had to cope with other traumatic events in their lives may have extra resilience, or they may be at more risk depending on other factors. In spite of all of these differences, there are many things we can do to minimize the negative effects of the trauma.

However, it is important to keep in mind that there are **no** coping methods that will make normal people feel *good* after traumatic, painful, or threatening situations. Therefore, our focus is on how to best cope with a legitimately difficult or unforeseen event. One important issue is that as human beings, *we like to be able to predict* what is going to happen to us. When we experience a highly unpredictable trauma, our sense of security is shattered. When we feel insecure, the normal anxieties of not knowing what will occur on a day-to-day basis tend to worsen. We tend to get fearful, as well as angry, with anyone who has taken away our security.

A second important issue that we have to confront in these times is the reality that we cannot control all of the risks in our lives. Just as we like **predictability**, we also like to maintain a sense of **control**. Whenever traumatic or major life events occur, it is a serious reminder that we cannot control everything that is important to us. Because some of these challenging events are sad or depressing as well as scary, we must be careful not to slip into a state of *helplessness* which would be detrimental to our health and well-being. The following set of recommendations can help you cope to some degree with the insecurity and emotional demands caused by these unpredictable and uncontrollable events.

## BEGINNING THE COPING PROCESS

If you have experienced a shared trauma such as a natural disaster or a violent incident, hopefully you have been fortunate enough to talk about the events in a critical incident stress group at school, at work, in your place of worship, or in your general community. If so, you have begun the healing process. If you have not had this opportunity, the following guidelines should be helpful.

### Talk about the event and your reactions.

Even if you do not have a formal group setting, it is important to talk about how you are reacting to the events. Keeping your fears to yourself is not likely to alleviate your stress. Withdrawal and avoidance of others may feel natural in these times, but this will slow your progress. Talk to family, teachers, friends, and other loved ones. Avoid isolating and keeping all of your feelings to yourself. It is helpful to hear from others you trust that they have some of the same feelings of vulnerability, anger, and sadness.

### Engage in self-care activities.

Taking care of some of your basic needs will make you more effective in your coping. Try to:

Get adequate rest and sleep, even though this can be difficult.
Drink plenty of non-alcoholic fluids, especially water.
Eat well.
Stay physically active, and exercise if possible - even if it is a brief walk.
Find a way to relax - listening to calming music, taking a warm bath, trying mindfulness or relaxation exercises, etc.
Distract yourself with pleasant activities - go to a movie, read pleasant books, go on-line, watch TV, etc.

Return to as much normal structure in your day as possible - normalize your school, work, and home routines as soon as you can. Limit exposure to news of the tragedy – you will want to stay informed, but avoid becoming obsessed with the event.

**Take control of whatever you can.**

In my consulting with various self-help groups such as AA and NA, I have been impressed with a philosophy about addictions that is very consistent with most psychological principles. These groups endorse the **Serenity Prayer**:

*God grant me the **serenity** to accept the things I cannot change;*
*the **courage** to change the things I can;*
*and the **wisdom** to know the difference.*

Whatever your religious beliefs may be, the important message here is that you will be in a better position if you focus on reminding yourself to take control of anything that is within your power to change. Frustration and disappointment are likely to be the outcomes when you are struggling to change things that are **not** within your control.

Feeling out of control is a very **unhealthy** emotion and can easily lead to anxiety, depression, and potentially dangerous *physiological* complications. It is important to remind yourself that even though you cannot control everything that is scary, you do have control over many other things. Avoid impulsive decisions that you may regret later. It is normal for anyone who is traumatized to feel vulnerable and want to escape the situation, such as your school or workplace if that's where a trauma occurred. You will need to determine when and how to return to scary places.

When a traumatic event does occur, it helps to take time to be with family or friends as a way to cope with the situation. Making these types of decisions promptly after an event can be important. However, at some point getting into anxiety provoking places where a trauma occurred can be necessary. Those who believe that their lives are being restricted in a negative way by a traumatic event might need outside help to overcome their fears.

## Minimize other changes or demands in your life.

Adding any significant changes in your life will create more stress. Therefore, it is wise whenever feasible not to take on new demands until the right time after a major life event occurs. This may not be possible after natural disasters, like Hurricane Katrina, where individuals were forced by the nature of the traumatic event to make drastic lifestyle adjustments quickly like moving to another city. In less dramatic situations, temporarily avoiding some stressful changes may be helpful until the period of uncertainty is over. This may mean postponing some changes, including even some things that would be considered positive stressors such as moving to a new house, taking on new responsibilities at your school or athletic teams, volunteering your time for extracurricular activities, etc.

## Find an active physical outlet to relieve some of the distress.

As discussed previously, stress can increase your frustration to the point that you become too irritable to brainstorm or consider all of your options. This may be the time to be sure you have some outlet for defusing your physical tension. Working out physically, hitting golf balls, playing tennis, basketball, or other active sports, going to sporting events as a spectator where you can yell for your team, will all be healthy ways to discharge tension. Even going for short walks or a bike ride in your neighborhood can be helpful if more strenuous activity is not feasible. If your stress is maintained over a lengthy period, it is wise to have a variety of these outlets available to get though these difficult times.

**Avoid the quick fixes.**

At these times, using alcohol, drugs, or food may seem tempting as an easier way to relieve your tension. However, these maladaptive coping methods, which might provide short-term relief, will cause additional problems in the long run. Again, if you find yourself relying on these methods to cope after a trauma, outside consultation with a professional could be helpful.

## OUR EXPERIENCE TELLS US

Healing is gradual after a major life event. Generally it takes a few weeks for things to begin to feel normal - in serious trauma it may take a lot longer. Do not place unrealistic expectations on yourself. Everyone will adjust to a traumatic event at his or her own pace. Normalizing your day-to-day activities is very important. Major life decisions can be postponed when possible and appropriate. Our sense of security might not return to its previous levels for some time. Any further incidents or reminders of our vulnerability will prolong this process. Use rational thoughts to remind yourself not to overreact.

You may find that you are more "edgy" or vigilant and react more strongly to sudden noises or other external stimuli. This is normal after we experience a trauma. However, you need to avoid becoming so sensitive that isolation and paranoia begins. The biggest challenge is to move beyond the immediate crisis stage when trauma occurs, and to begin to cope with the event in a positive way. By doing this you may be able to find some relief from the most intense feelings associated with the event. Remember not to expect anyone to make you feel comfortable about these major life events. This will not happen. You can, however, find ways to relieve the intensity of your emotional pain and to minimize the impact of these events on the rest of your life.

If the level of distress seems unbearable for too long, consider a consultation with a professional. Sometimes the issues are so complicated that having a counselor or therapist as a resource will help you handle the stressful events more quickly and effectively. This may be particularly important for those who have a personal history of other tragedies in their lives. In cases where your functioning is impaired or you sense that your health is at risk, it is also advisable to consult with your physician regarding possible medications that are sometimes helpful.

Many of the recommendations listed above are practical in nature. Following these guidelines can be helpful in buffering yourself from the immediate trauma and its resulting changes in your lives. However, trauma specialists often remind victims and rescue workers that they can be forever changed by these events. Once people experience severe trauma, they cannot perceive the world in the same way that they did prior to the traumatic event. Although you may never forget the event, this does not mean that you will be "traumatized" forever. We may see the world as less secure and less predictable. We need to find some way to gain a new and healthy perspective that makes sense to us, and that allows us to function well in spite of any new worries and anxieties.

There is no single prescription regarding how to do this. Some will find their answers through self-reflection and discussions with family and friends. Some may need guidance from their spiritual leaders to accept what happened and move on with life. Still others will find help through therapy to integrate these new experiences into their lives in such a way that the negative impact is minimized. Try to find an approach that fits your personal values and situation.

# Summary of iCope Procedures

The basic **iCope** procedures are summarized here in this reduced format for your personal use. It is recommended that you make copies that can be saved and used as reminders in various ways. For example, have copies laminated and used as bookmarks, or keep a copy folded in your wallet or book bag as a reminder to practice.

1. **TUNE INTO YOUR STRESS LEVEL**. Improve your self-awareness. Rate your stress from **1** (very relaxed) to **10** (very stressed). Whenever you feel tense, proceed with the rest of the steps.

2. **RELAX!** Take a deep breath that extends your stomach, hold it for 4-5 seconds, breathe out slowly through your mouth while saying "calm" or "cope" to yourself. Repeat this a second time.

3. **TALK RATIONALLY TO YOURSELF**. "What's making me so stressed? It's probably not as bad as I think. I've handled situations like this before. I can calm myself and feel better later." Challenge any of your *irrational* beliefs. Avoid negative mental habits such as overgeneralizing, catastrophizing, or focusing on the negative. Be positive and keep things in perspective.

4. **PROBLEM SOLVE**. Think about your options. Avoid saying "*nothing can be done*." Be an *active coper* and take control of whatever you can. What can you do soon to feel better without getting yourself into trouble? Pick an option and try it. If it doesn't help, try another until you feel better. Stay flexible and be creative.

5. **RECHECK YOUR STRESS LEVEL**. If you reduced your stress, even slightly, take credit for a job well done. Check to see if you reached your *effective stress zone*. If your stress remains high, remind yourself it takes practice, and go back to Step 2 and repeat the procedure. With practice you will get better.

# References and Suggested Readings

As mentioned in the Preface, there is a vast literature on stress management. A Google search in February 2012 listed over 119 million hits for "stress" and 20 million for "stress management." Because there are so many specific books on stress management and its related topics, it is impossible to give the reader a comprehensive reading list. However, a sampling of some of the books that supplement our procedures is presented below. I also encourage the reader to use the internet to look for topics of high interest and on-going research such as specific health concerns or illnesses that are affected by stress, Type D personality factors, and relevant lifestyle issues such as fitness and nutrition that affect our resilience to stress. Also check out **http://www.icope.co** for current developments, free worksheets, and supplemental materials related to improving coping skills.

## STRESS, HEALTH & WELLNESS

*One Minute Stress Management: Easy Strategies to Conquer Stress*, by A. R. Ciminero, iUniverse, 2006.

*Managing Stress: Principles and Strategies for Health and Well-Being (Fifth Edition)*, by Brian Luke Seaward, Jones and Bartlett Publishers, 2006.

*Stress & Health: Biological and Psychological Interactions (Second Edition),* by William R. Lovallo, Sage Publications, 2005.

*The Stress of Life* (Revised Ed.), by H. Selye, McGraw-Hill, 1978.

*Stress Management: A Comprehensive Guide to Wellness,* by E. Charlesworth & R. Nathan, Atheneum, 1985.

## RELAXATION METHODS

*The Relaxation Response,* by H. Benson, Avon Books, 1975.

*The Relaxation and Stress Reduction Workbook, 3rd Ed.,* by M. Davis, E.R. Eshelman, & M. McKay, New Harbinger Publications, 1988.

## COGNITIVE RESTRUCTURING

*A New Guide to Rational Living,* by A. Ellis & R.A. Harper, Wilshire Book Co., 1975.

*Rational Behavior Therapy,* by M. Maultsby, Prentice-Hall, 1984.

*The Feeling Good Handbook,* by D. Burns, Plume, 1990.

## ASSERTIVENESS & ANGER MANAGEMENT

*Responsible Assertive Behavior,* by A. Lange & P. Jakawbawski, Research Press, 1979.

*When Anger Hurts: Quieting the Storm Within,* by M. McKay, P.D. Rogers, & J. McKay, New Harbinger Publications, 1989.

## SELF ESTEEM AND CONFIDENCE

*Ten Days to Self-Esteem,* by David D. Burns, HarperCollins Publishers, *1993*.

*The Self-Esteem Workbook,* by G.R. Schiraldi, New Harbinger Publications, 2000.

*Think Confident, Be Confident,* by L. Sokol & M. Fox, Perigee, 2009.

## MINDFULNESS AND POSITIVE PSYCHOLOGY

*Fully Present: The Science, Art, and Practice of Mindfulness,* by S. L. Smalley & D. Winston, Da Capo Press, 2010.

*Mindfulness for Beginners: reclaiming the present moment - and your life,* by Jon Kabat-Zinn, Sounds True, Inc., 2012.

*A Mindfulness-Based Stress Reduction Workbook,* by B. Stahl & E. Goldstein, New Harbinger Publications, 2010.

*Flourish,* by M.E.P. Seligman, Free Press, 2011.

*The Stress Reduction Workbook for Teens: Mindfulness Skills to Help You Deal With Stress,* by G. Biegel, Instant Help Books - A Division of New Harbinger Publications, 2009.

## QR CODE FOR OUR WEBSITE

**Use your Smart Phone QR App to use this Code to go to:
http://www.icope.co**